D1249714

## Living Things

Exploring and Understanding Plant Structure
Exploring and Understanding Plant Functions
Exploring and Understanding Insects
Exploring and Understanding Fish
Exploring and Understanding Birds
Exploring and Understanding Amphibians and Reptiles
Exploring and Understanding Mammals
Exploring and Understanding the Human Body

## Earth and the Universe

Exploring and Understanding Air
Exploring and Understanding Soil
Exploring and Understanding Water
Exploring and Understanding Rocks and Minerals
Exploring and Understanding Weather and Climate
Exploring and Understanding Our Changing Earth
Exploring and Understanding Our Solar System
Exploring and Understanding Beyond the Solar System

## Matter and Energy

Exploring and Understanding Machines
Exploring and Understanding Light
Exploring and Understanding Electricity
Exploring and Understanding Sound
Exploring and Understanding Heat
Exploring and Understanding Magnets and Electromagnets
Exploring and Understanding Rockets and Satellites
Exploring and Understanding Chemistry

EDWARD VICTOR
Consulting Science Editor
Northwestern University

*Exploring and Understanding*

# OUR SOLAR SYSTEM



by

DAN Q. POSIN

SAN FRANCISCO STATE COLLEGE

BENEFIC PRESS • WESTCHESTER, ILLINOIS

# CONTENTS



Library of Congress
Number 68-15585

**Cover Photo: The Planet Saturn**

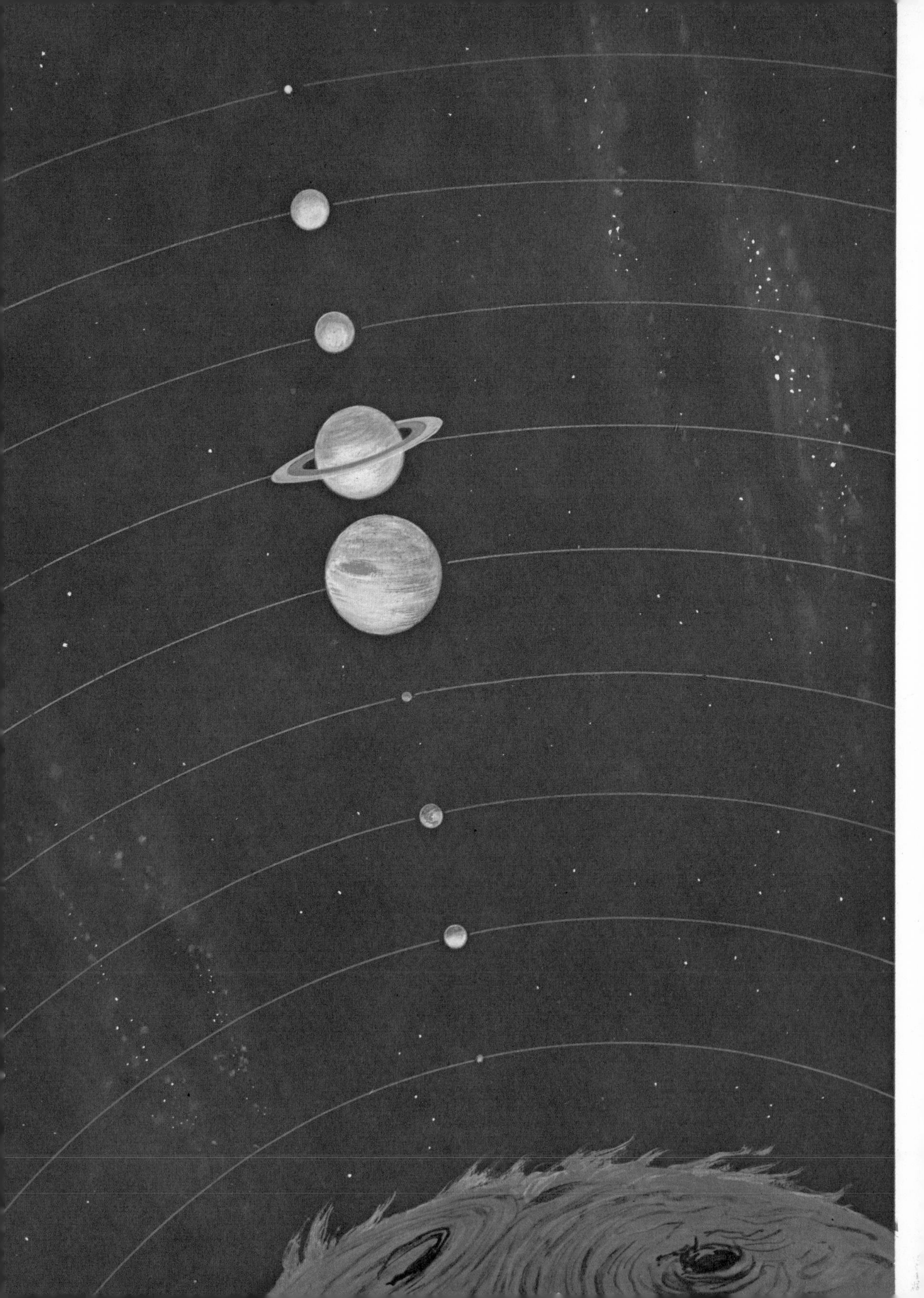

# THE ORIGIN OF THE SOLAR SYSTEM

Our Earth is only one of a large group of objects which move together through space. We call this group the *solar system*. Our own star, the Sun, gives heat and light to its family of nine *planets* as they move around the Sun, each in its own path at its own speed. The planets do not produce their own light, but shine only because the light of the Sun falls upon them. Earth is one of these planets, and if you were out in space, you would see it shining too. Most of the planets have *moons*, smaller objects which move around the planet as it moves around the Sun. Our Earth has only one moon.

In addition to the Sun, planets, and moons of our solar system, there are many rocks or pieces of iron flying around the Sun -- the *meteors*. There are also many shiny, gassy-looking bodies, called *comets*, which wander around our Sun. Comets are seen in our sky only once in a while, but there are many of them. Because all these objects are seen in the sky, they are called *celestial* bodies.

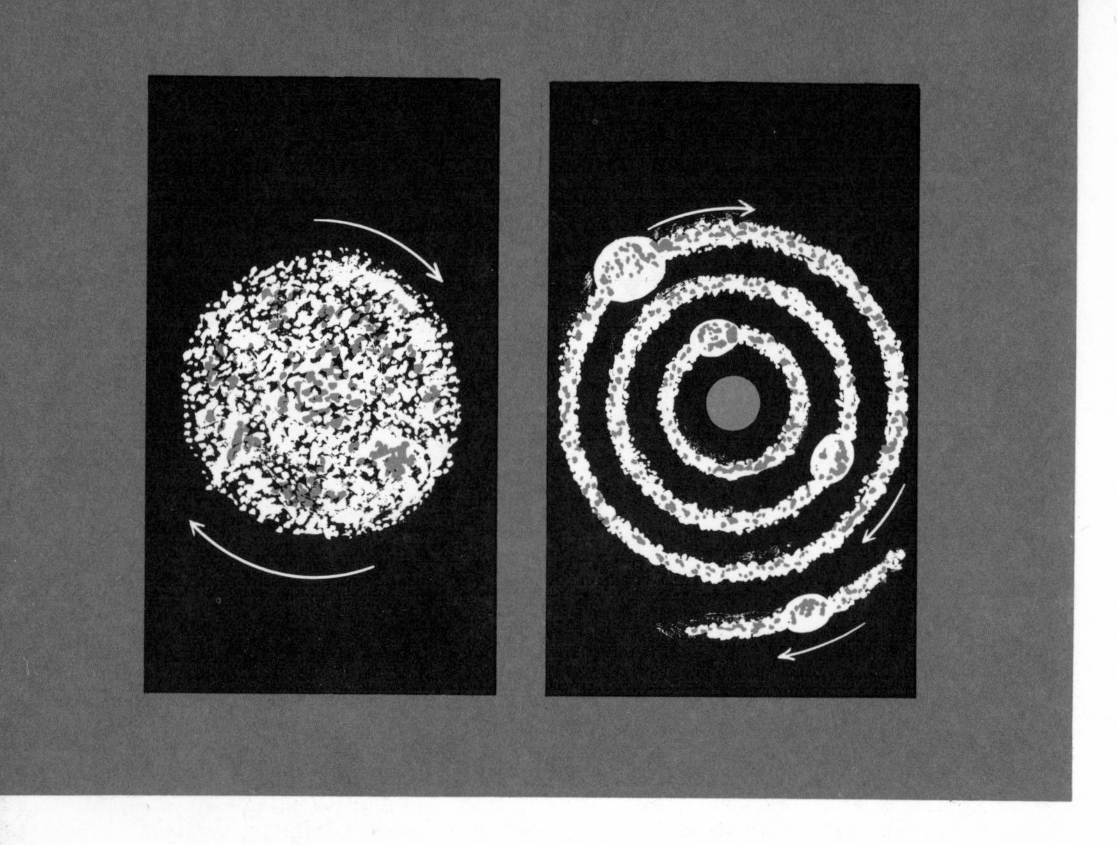

**How Did the System Begin?**

There are several ideas about the origin, or beginning, of the solar system.

Many years ago, the German philosopher, Immanuel Kant, and the French scientist, Pierre Simon de Laplace, believed that the planets came into being at the same time as the Sun, and that it was all part of the same event. Kant and Laplace believed that once upon a time, in space, there was a rotating cloud of cool and thin gas. Do you remember that everything has gravity and pulls on everything else near it? Gravity pulled the central part of this gas together over a long period of time. This central part became the Sun. Other parts of the uneven rotating cloud pulled together and got smaller and denser. In other words, the gas *condensed* into separate clumps at different distances from the Sun. These clumps became the nine planets, and smaller clumps became moons.

James Clerk Maxwell, a scientist who studied how matter behaved, did not agree with the idea, or theory, of Kant and Laplace. He had worked out a mathematical demonstration about Saturn. He showed that Saturn's rings had never come together into a couple of moons, because the force of gravity between the particles was not strong enough. Therefore, Maxwell said, the rings would stay forever. He pointed out that according to the Kant-Laplace theory, the future planets would have been rings around the Sun like the rings around Saturn, but that they would never have condensed to form planets.

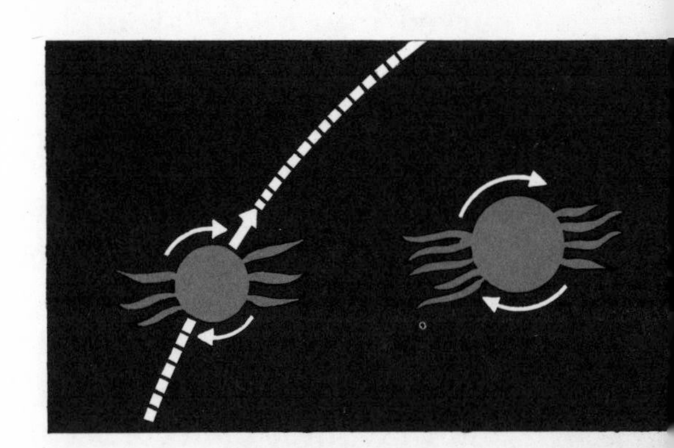

#### What Was the Collision Theory?

A new idea was then developed called the collision theory. In this theory, scientists thought that our Sun and another star had come close to each other in space. The second star pulled material out of our Sun. The material circled in blobs around our Sun and condensed into planets.

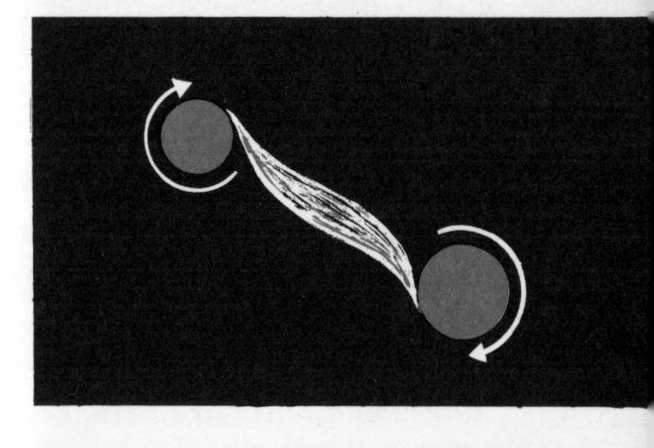

This theory did not seem to explain all the facts and was soon dropped. For one thing, it could not explain why the planets have almost circular paths, or *orbits*.

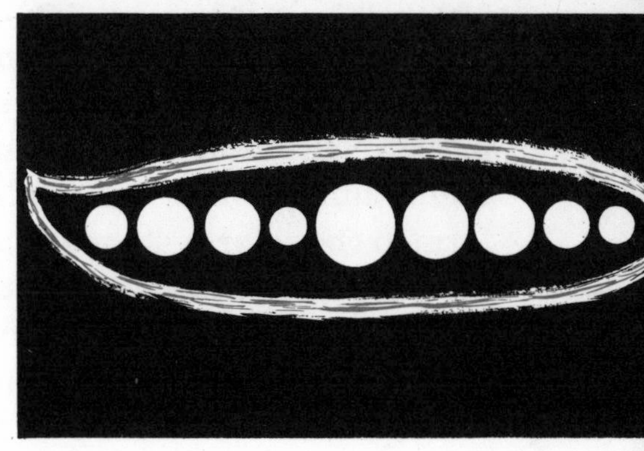

Another theory much like the collision theory was proposed by scientist Fred Hoyle. His theory was that the Sun was once a double star. That is, he thought the Sun had a companion star as many stars do. He thought the companion star had exploded and sent material flying by the Sun. The material curved into orbits around the Sun and became the planets.

**Why Was Maxwell Wrong?**

The scientists learned something that made them take another look at Maxwell's objection to the Kant-Laplace theory. Remember he thought that the pull of gravity could not be strong enough to pull the small bits, or particles, together to form planets. Scientists have known for a long time that all substances are made up of tiny particles called *molecules* and that these molecules can be divided into even smaller bits called *atoms.* Some materials have different kinds of atoms. Some have all the same kind. The materials with only one kind of atoms are known as *elements.*

When James Maxwell objected to the Kant-Laplace theory, he had thought that the elements found in the largest amounts on Earth would also be found in the largest amounts on the Sun. He thought the Sun had quite a lot of iron, oxygen, silicon, and other elements found in large amounts on Earth. These elements are called heavy elements because their atoms are heavy. Scientists have now learned that the Sun does not have many of the heavy elements. The Sun and stars are made mostly of hydrogen and helium. These two elements have very light-weight atoms. Since the Sun is made of mostly hydrogen and helium, scientists are almost certain that the cloud which formed the solar system was made up mostly of these two light-weight elements with only small amounts of the heavy elements. The cloud would have to have been much larger than they first thought to have enough heavy elements to form the planets of the solar system.

What does this mean? It means that if this cloud was so large, then the pull of gravity would be stronger than Maxwell thought. It would be strong enough to pull the particles together into separate clumps.

These early clumps of hydrogen, helium and a few heavier atoms, have been named *protoplanets*. They kept changing as time passed. The heavier atoms, such as iron and cobalt, settled toward the center. They became the solid part of the planet. The lighter gas became the atmosphere around the solid part.

Although the Sun got a head start on the planets, it was not yet fully formed. It was a huge ball that was condensing and getting warm. When the Sun finally became more condensed as it is today, it began to *radiate*, or send out, lots of energy, such as light, gamma rays, and X rays. The rays blew away much of the thinner outer atmosphere around the planets. The planets, for a while, may have looked like a bunch of comets, with thin bright tails blowing away in a direction opposite to the sun. When the tails of hydrogen and helium had been blown away, the harder part of the planets was left.

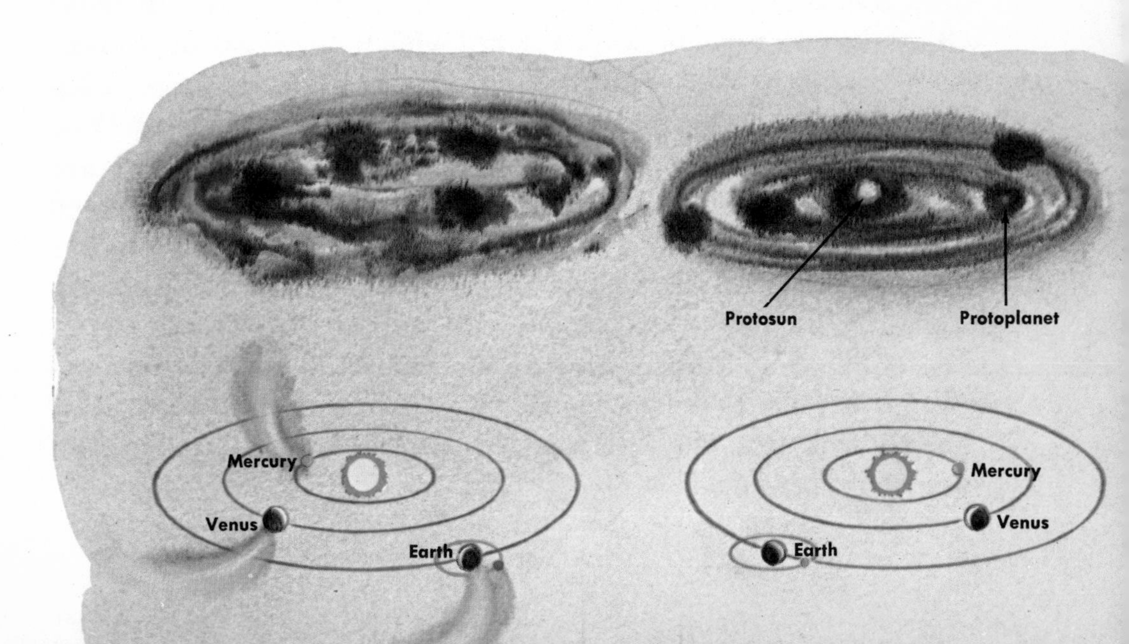

Mercury, Venus, Earth, and Mars, the planets closest to the Sun, had all of their atmosphere blown away. All but Mercury developed new atmospheres later from their rocky surfaces. The planets further from the Sun did not lose all their first atmospheres. Their atmospheres are still mostly hydrogen.

### Are There Other Solar Systems?

Astronomers have found that stars often explode and send out big clouds of hydrogen. It is quite usual to have big clouds of gas rotating in space. Each one of these might become a solar system. Therefore, we can expect a tremendous number of solar systems in space. In fact, we do believe that most stars have a number of planets. Do you believe that in the other solar systems there might be planets with conditions enough like our planet so that there could be life on them?

### Why Do Planets Orbit Around Their Sun?

The planets have already been traveling around the Sun for about five billion years. What keeps them there? Why don't they fall into the Sun? Or, why don't they fly away?

To understand the answer to these questions, you must know two things about moving objects. You know that gravity will make two objects move toward each other if nothing stops them. Since the Sun is larger than Earth, the Earth would fall straight toward the Sun if the Earth were not moving. Why does the movement of the Earth make a difference? Have you ever swung a ball around on a string? What happened when you let go of the string? The ball flew off in a straight line, didn't it? Anything that is moving in a straight line will keep moving in a straight line unless something interferes. Therefore, gravity keeps pulling the Earth toward the Sun and the moving Earth keeps trying to move off in a straight line. The result is that the Earth moves around the Sun in a curved almost circular path.

A look at the diagram will show you why. Let's say the Earth started at point $a$. If the Sun were not present, the Earth would move in a straight line. Let's say it would arrive at point $b$ in one day. However, the Sun is present and the gravity of the Sun has pulled on the Earth enough so it would have fallen from point $b$ to point $c$ in one day. Instead of moving straight ahead and then falling, the Earth is falling a little bit all the time it is going ahead. It really arrives at point $c$ by traveling in a curved path to get there. The Earth keeps moving in a curved path all the way around the Sun. Of course, this is true of all the other planets which are orbiting the Sun.

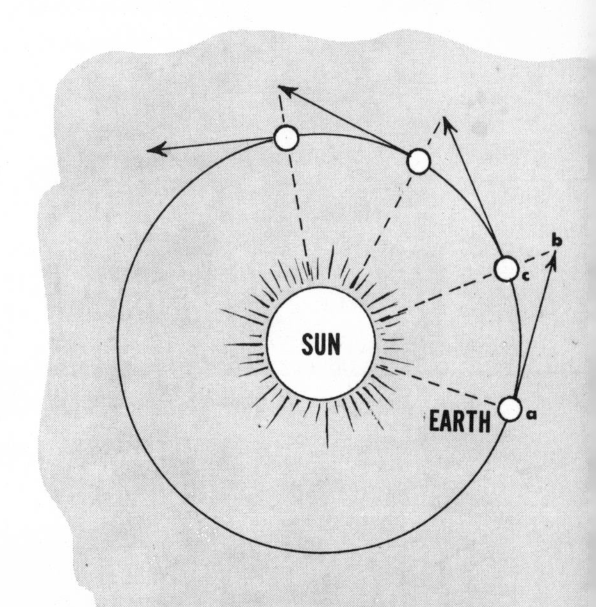

## Things to Think About

1. Is a moon a planet? Explain your answer.

2. What is a protoplanet?

3. What is in our solar system?

4. What is an element? What are the two most common light-weight elements found in the Sun? Why are they light in weight?

5. Why does the Moon orbit the Earth? What keeps it from flying away?

6. What is a collision? If you do not know, look it up in the dictionary. Do you think the name "collision theory" is a good name for that theory about the solar system?

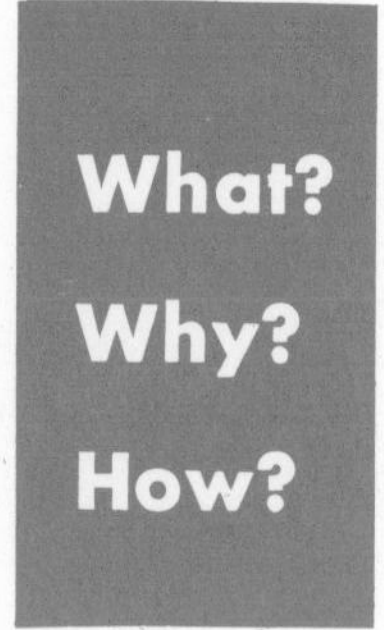


Hold a ball made of crushed aluminum foil in your hand. Let go of it. How does it move? What causes it to move that way?

Now, fasten the ball to a string. Go outdoors and swing the ball on the string. Let go. Watch carefully how the ball moves. Does this demonstrate a planet in orbit?

# OUR STAR -- THE SUN

The stars in the sky are sizzling-hot balls of flaming gas. Some of these fiery spheres are only a few thousand miles in *diameter*, which means the measurement from one side to the other through the center. Others are many millions of miles in diameter. Our Sun, which is a star, is a fairly small star. It is only about 865,000 miles in diameter. Still, it is so large that more than a million Earths could be dropped inside. Why do you suppose our Sun looks so large compared to other larger stars? Of course, this is because it is so close to us. It is only about 93,000,000 miles away. The next nearest star to us, Proxima Centauri, is about 24,000,000,000,000 miles from us. That is more than 250,000 times further away. Is it any wonder that our star seems so much larger than all others?

The Sun is always in a state of violent action. The heat of the Sun causes the surface to bubble and boil. It flares up, and then simmers down. Long flames shoot out into space. Gigantic spots appear at times on the Sun's surface.

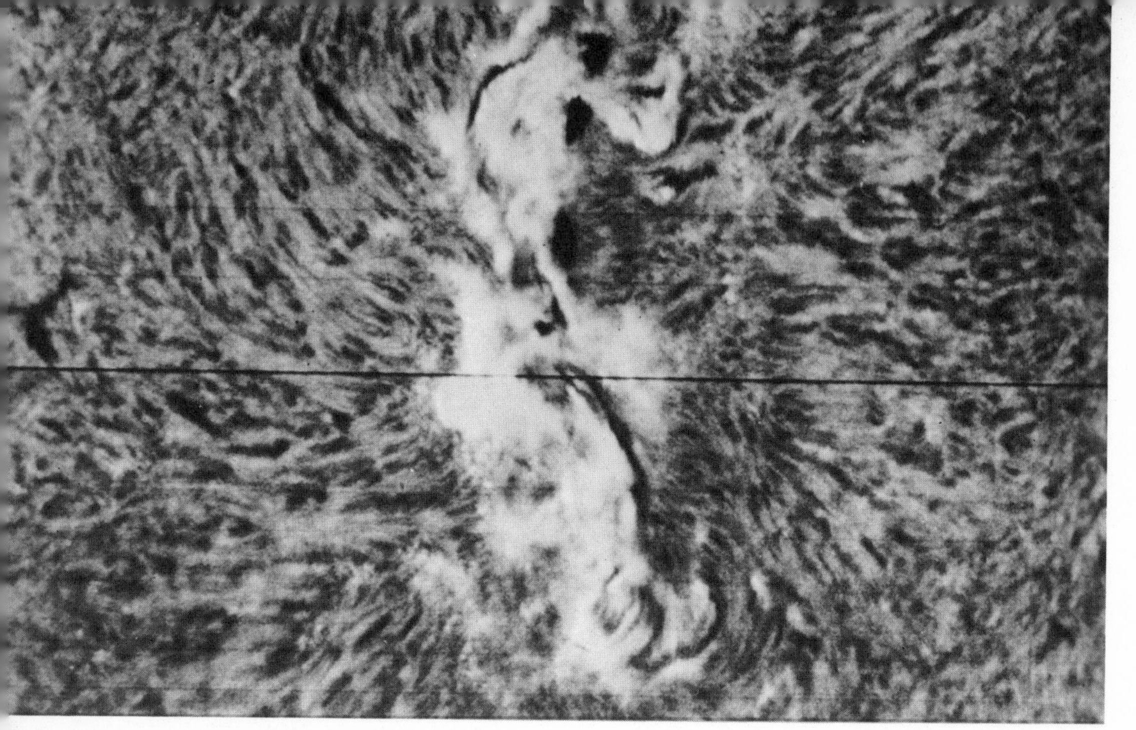

**Surface of the Sun**

### How Dense Is the Sun?

Astronomers have been able to determine the mass of the Sun, and they know how much space it takes up. They are then able to measure the *density* of the Sun. Density is the amount of mass or matter in a certain amount of space. The density of the Sun is about 100 pounds per cubic foot. A cubic foot is a cube that is one foot long, one foot wide, and one foot high. The density of water is 62.4 pounds per cubic foot, so you can get an idea of how dense the Sun is. This figure is the average density; the density is not the same all over the Sun. Where do you think it would be the most dense? Actually, near the center of the Sun, the density is about 6000 pounds per cubic foot.

### How Hot Is the Sun?

Astronomers have been able to measure the temperature of the surface of the Sun. They think the sun's surface is about 10,000 degrees Fahrenheit. The temperature of gases around the Sun may be as hot as 4 million degrees Fahrenheit.

**What Are the Parts of the Sun?**

Astronomers who study the Sun are able to see only the outside part. They can measure the temperature of the surface and see how the gases of its atmosphere move. However, these scientists have been able to figure out what probably happens on the inside of the Sun and what it looks like.

The core, or center, of the Sun is where the sun's energy starts. That is where hydrogen atoms are fused, or joined together, to make helium atoms. The core is surrounded by an area that is a little cooler, but it is an area where the Sun's energy is working toward the surface.

That hot area is surrounded by the *photosphere.* This is the part that can be seen on the surface of the Sun. It is the part that bubbles and boils.

There is a very thin layer around the photosphere called the *chromosphere.* It separates the very hot *corona* from the photosphere which is cooler. The part of the Sun named corona is the part that can be seen when there is a total *solar eclipse,* which occurs when the Moon is in a position so it hides the Sun. The corona looks like a halo around the Sun. The temperature in the gases of the corona is surprisingly high. It is 3 to 4 million degrees Fahrenheit. Scientists believe this high temperature may be due to the noisy rumbling sound of the Sun's hot boiling surface. The sound energy becomes heat energy when it is absorbed by the corona gases which are thus heated to a high temperature.

Scientists studying the surface of the Sun can see bright, hot areas which they call *plages.* There are also *sunspots* which are dark, cool areas on the surface. *Prominences* can also be seen. These are like large mountains of gas which shoot up out of the corona and then die down again.

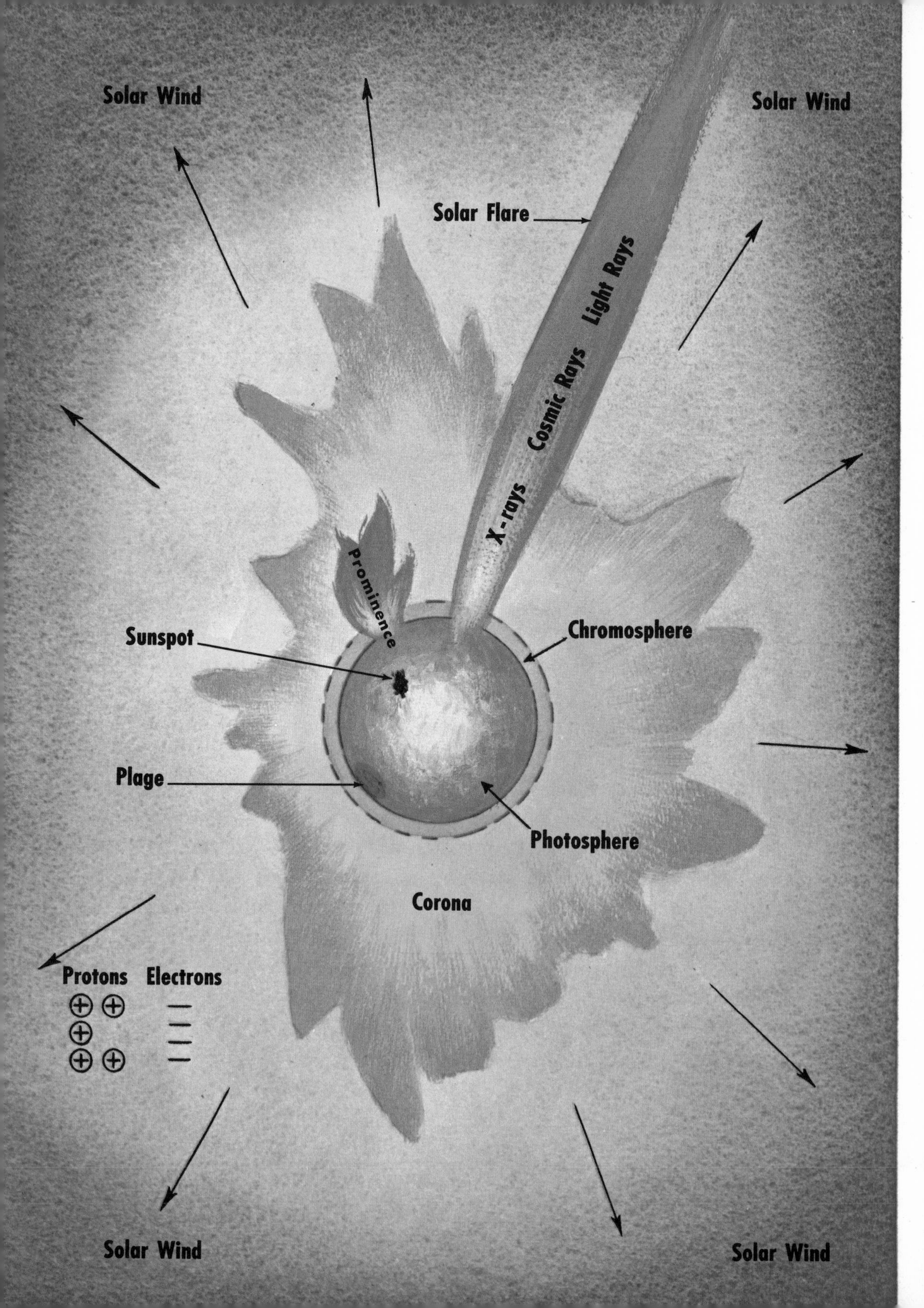

Solar Wind
Solar Wind
Solar Flare
Light Rays
Cosmic Rays
X-rays
Prominence
Sunspot
Chromosphere
Plage
Photosphere
Corona
Protons
Electrons
Solar Wind
Solar Wind

### How Is the Temperature of the Sun Measured?

Do you wonder how the temperature of the Sun can be measured so far away? Have you ever used a prism to break white light into rainbow colors, or colors of the *spectrum*? These colors go from red to violet in a certain order. Scientists can tell many things by studying the spectrum of sunlight. First, here on Earth, light from glowing objects of different temperatures is broken into its spectrum and photographed. By comparing these with pictures of spectrums of light from the Sun, scientists can tell the temperature of different parts of the Sun.

### Does the Sun Have a Magnetic Field?

If you have experimented with magnets, you have probably used iron filings to show lines of force between the N and S poles of the magnet. We know that the Earth is just like a big magnet. It has a north magnetic pole and a south magnetic pole, and there are lines of magnetic force in between these poles. The area which is affected by these lines of force is called a *magnetic field.*

Does the Sun have a magnetic field similar to the Earth? The scientists wanted to know. They found out by experimenting with light. Again, here on Earth, experiments were done with light and magnetism to see what would happen. The scientists found that magnetism will cause certain colors to split up, as they do when light passes through a prism. The stronger the magnetic field, the more the colors separate.

Then the scientists examined the Sun's light to see how much the colors separated. They found out that the separation effect was very strong, and so decided that the Sun has magnetic fields thousands of times stronger than those on the Earth.

The light that comes from sunspots often shows a very strong separation effect due to magnetism. The sunspots nearly always appear in pairs. One sunspot is toward a magnetic north and the other toward a magnetic south. You could say that the sunspots are storms which rage between pairs of poles of magnets within the Sun. There are many such pairs, but they do not stay in one place.

What actually produces this magnetism? It is produced by electric currents on the Sun. The Sun does have positive and negative electrical charges. All atoms have particles called *protons*, which have a positive charge, and lighter-weight particles called *electrons*, which have a negative charge. The electrons move much more freely than the protons and may move from one atom to another.

When a substance has many electrons it is said to have a negative electrical charge. The electrons will move to substances that have a shortage of electrons. A substance with a shortage of electrons is said to have a positive charge. This movement of electrons is an electric current. An electric current always has a magnetic field around it. A wire with an electric current moving through it would have magnetic lines of force as shown in the diagram.

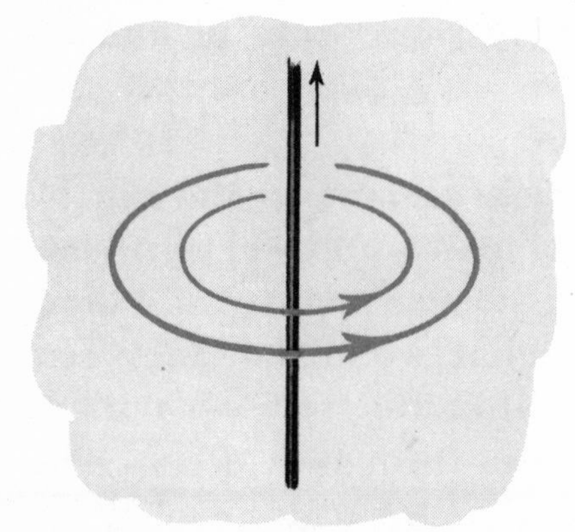

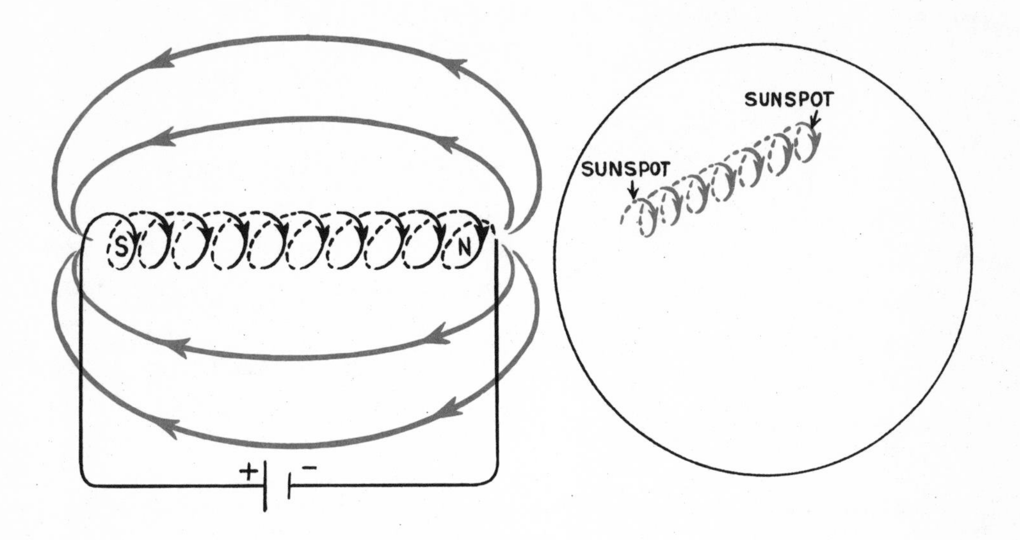


This is what may happen on the Sun. Hot electrically charged gases below the surface flow up and down. The *rotation*, or turning, of the Sun turns them a little and makes loops of electric current which burst through the surface. These loops with an electric current produce a magnetic field. The sunspots then are really electrical storms which cause strong magnetic lines of force.

When the Sun is especially active and hurls its flames into space, the magnetic disturbance travels through space and affects the magnetism over the Earth. It disturbs the magnetic fields of Earth and makes radio communication bad. It causes the northern lights, called *aurora borealis*, and the southern lights, called *aurora australis*. The disturbances are called solar storms and they occur in 11 1/2 year cycles. In other words, it takes about 11 1/2 years for the Sun to change from a period with many sunspots, to a period with only a few, and then back again to many sunspots.

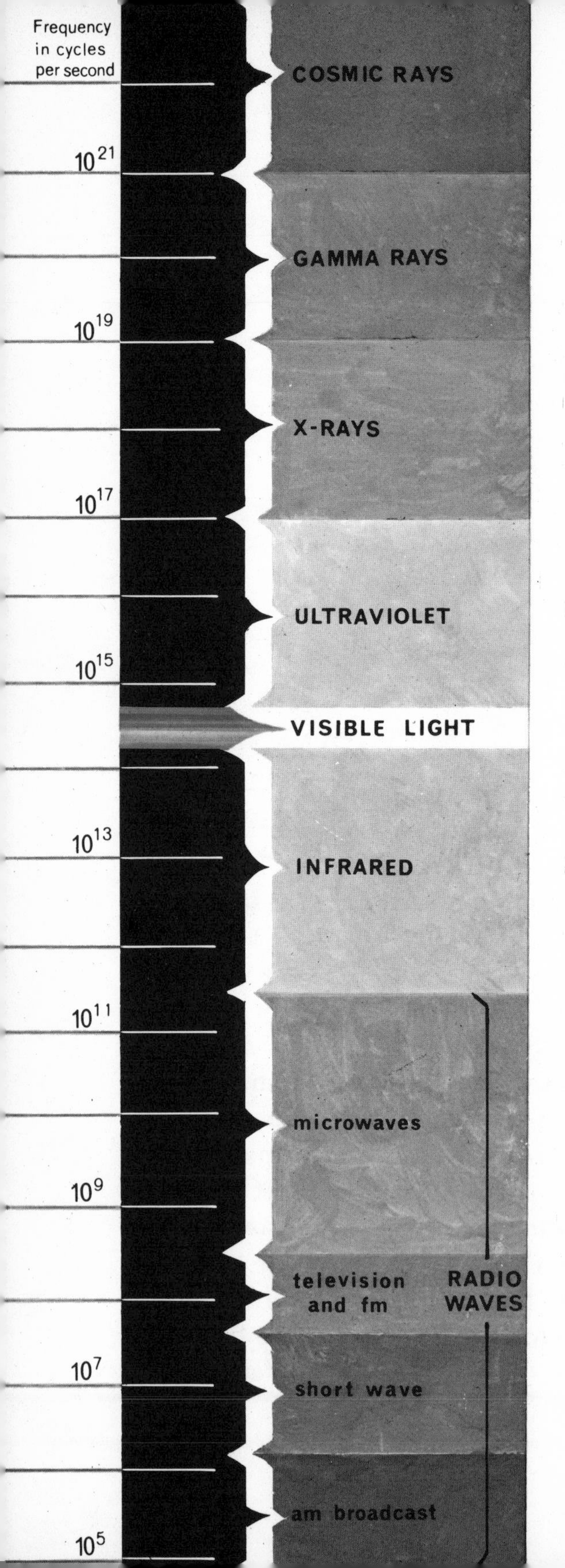


**What Kinds of Waves Reach the Earth From the Sun?**

The sound waves which are produced by the Sun cannot go beyond the corona because there is empty space, or a *vacuum* further out. Sound cannot travel through a vacuum. Other waves, which are radio type waves, do reach us from the Sun. They can travel through a vacuum more easily than through air.

The waves, called *electromagnetic*, travel away from the Sun with the speed of light -- about 186,000 miles per second. They are produced whenever electrical particles suddenly speed up or slow down. The waves must be produced on the Sun whenever its streaming charged gases speed up or slow down.

These waves have different frequencies. *Frequency* is the number of waves that are produced in one second. The arrangement of these waves from highest to lowest frequency is also called a *spectrum*. The visible light spectrum is part of the larger spectrum.

In addition to the electromagnetic waves, which are simply traveling effects without matter, the Sun does fire out some particles. These are the positively charged protons and the negatively charged electrons. The particles travel across the vacuum of space at great speeds but not as fast as light. The magnetic field of the Earth turns these charged particles toward the north and south magnetic poles. They cause an electric discharge in our upper atmosphere that produces the aurora borealis and aurora australis near the north and south poles.

**What Makes the Inside of the Sun so Hot?**

The temperatures inside the Sun have, of course, not been measured. They are merely figured out, or *calculated*. How do you suppose this is done? The scientists first figure how *compressed*, or squeezed, the Sun's gaseous material is at different levels. Then they can figure how much the temperature goes up. If you compress a gas, the temperature goes up. When you pump up a bicycle tire rapidly, feel the pump tube and see if it gets warmer. Since the compression is greater nearer the center of the Sun, the Sun is also much denser near the center.

**How Much Energy Does the Sun Produce?**

The amount of energy that falls on one square foot on Earth can be measured. Let's use a calorie for the unit of heat measure. One *calorie* is the amount of heat energy necessary to change the temperature of one gram (a very small amount) of water by one degree Centigrade. By using the amount of calories that falls on one square foot and the distance of the Sun which is 93,000,000 miles away, the total energy that it radiates can be calculated. The total energy radiated by the Sun turns out to be $10^{26}$ calories per second. (You may know that this figure is 1 followed by 26 zeros, or 100,000,000,000,000,000,000,000,000 calories per second.)

### How Does the Sun Produce Its Energy?

At one time, scientists believed that the Sun produced its energy by ordinary burning of some material. Calculations, however, showed that if the Sun burned any fuel, such as gasoline or coal, the Sun would burn out completely in a few thousand years. But how long has the Sun been burning brightly? For about five billion years.

There was another theory that the Sun's energy came from contracting, or becoming smaller, due to gravity pulling the matter inward. Such squeezing together, or compression, would produce some heat, but it would only be enough to allow the Sun to shine forth for two or three hundred million years.

Another suggestion was that the Sun's energy comes from *radioactivity* which is the giving off of little bursts of energy and fast-moving particles by such substances as radium, uranium, and thorium. It is true that a great deal of heat energy can come from radioactivity, but in a natural state, this would be a very slow process. To get as much heat as the Sun puts out, it would have to be made almost entirely of radioactive materials. But it isn't. By studying the Sun's colors as seen through a prism, we learn that the Sun is mostly ordinary hydrogen gas, which is not radioactive.

The present accepted theory is that the Sun's energy must come from some speeded-up nuclear process. Probably the high temperatures of millions of degrees cause a faster nuclear reaction. One of the nuclear reactions in the Sun is the changing of hydrogen gas into helium plus a burst of energy. The *nucleus*, or central portion, of a hydrogen atom consists of only one proton. The fast-moving hydrogen nuclei collide with each other, join together, and lose some of their mass. The process of joining together is called *fusion*. The lost mass becomes energy such as X-rays, gamma rays, and sunlight.

This is what happens in a hydrogen-helium reaction.

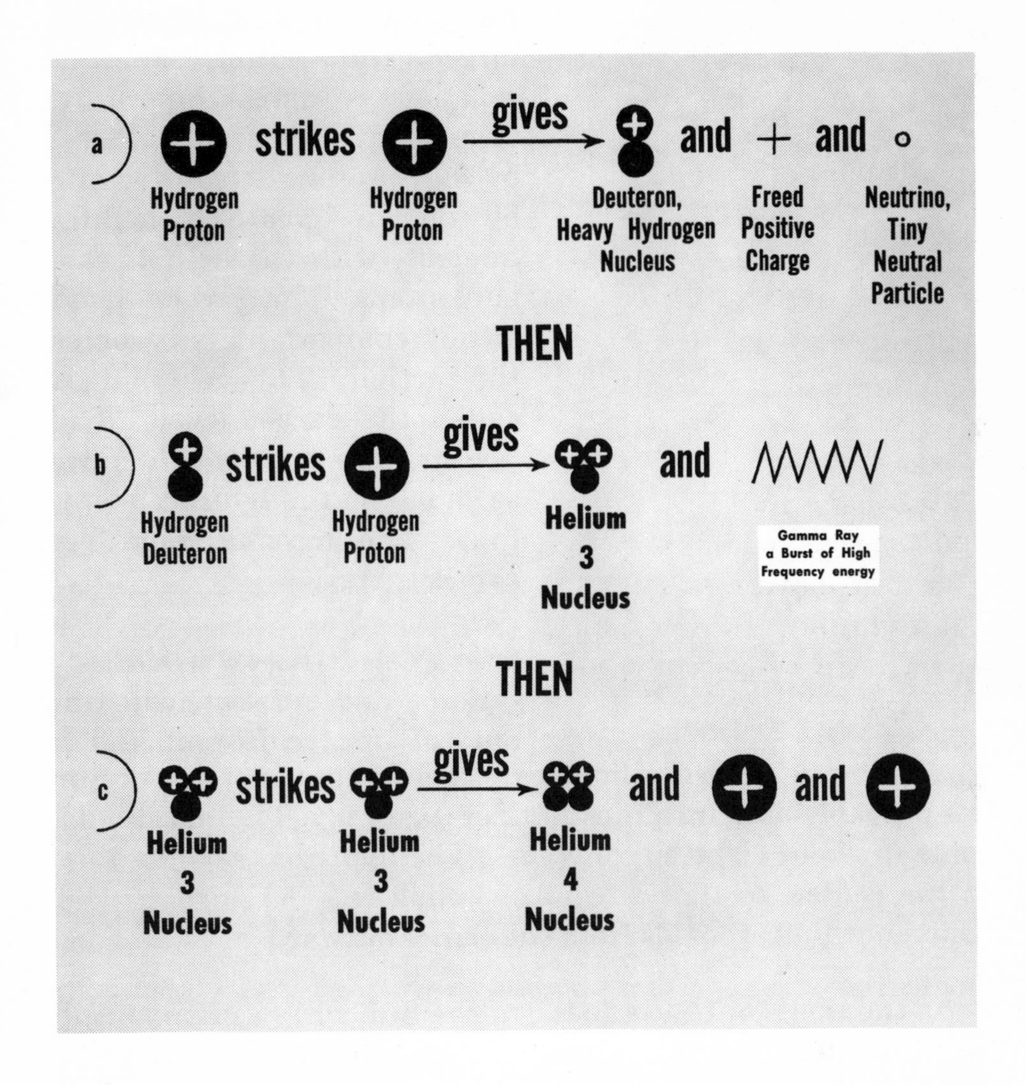


Notice that first there is a building up of *deuterons* from protons, then a build-up of helium-3 nuclei from deuterons and more protons; and finally, a build-up of helium-4 (ordinary helium) from helium-3 particles. The result is that hydrogen has been changed into helium, and energy has been given off. And so it goes, with countless particles, over and over.

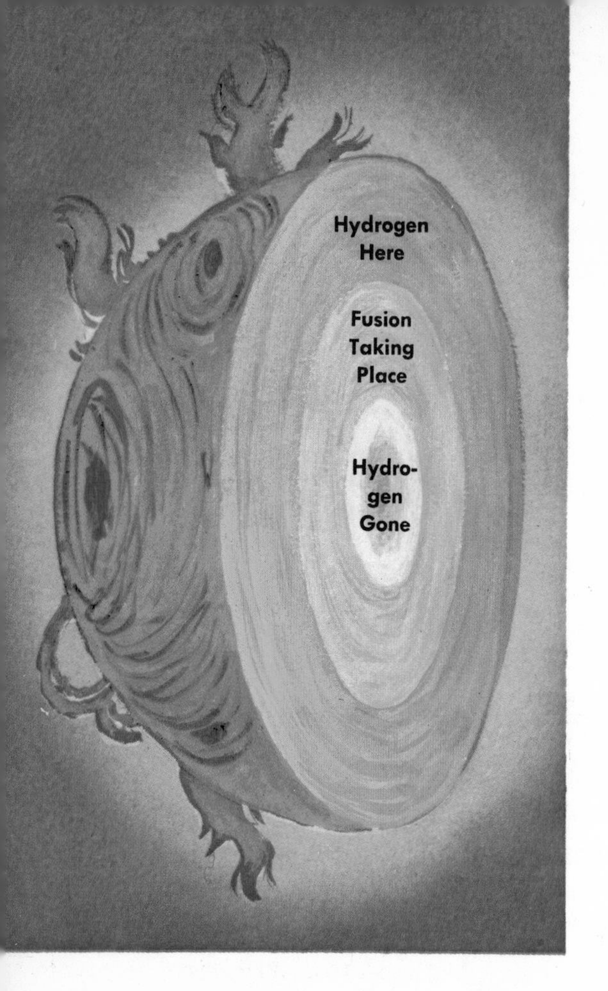


The hydrogen-helium reaction is the chief one for our Sun; but in stars that are larger and hotter, another reaction is more important. It is a series of events whereby four protons are united one by one to create a helium nucleus, with the help of carbon atoms. The carbon itself is not changed; it only helps the action. The reaction is called the carbon cycle. The helium does not weigh quite as much as the hydrogen protons. The missing mass becomes energy.

**What Is Going to Happen to Our Sun?**

Some day our Sun will run out of its hydrogen. Then what? Now, after five billion years of giving out energy, our Sun has probably used up almost half of its supply. The end should come in about eight billion years. The hydrogen gets used up at the center, so that a kind of hollowness develops, as the fusion burning proceeds from the center outward.

As the shell continues to burn, the Sun will swell and begin to shine more. It will continue to swell although it is running out of hydrogen. After several hundred million years, the Sun will have swollen so large that it will have swallowed up Mercury and Venus, and it will be expanding toward Earth. The Earth's water will boil away. When it begins to get too warm, do you think the Earth people will get into their spaceships and go to that nice warm planet of Pluto?

Now, the Sun will run out of hydrogen, begin to cool, and contract, or get smaller. The contraction fires up the inside with renewed heat. This starts a new nuclear reaction. Helium nuclei unite to form carbon nuclei.

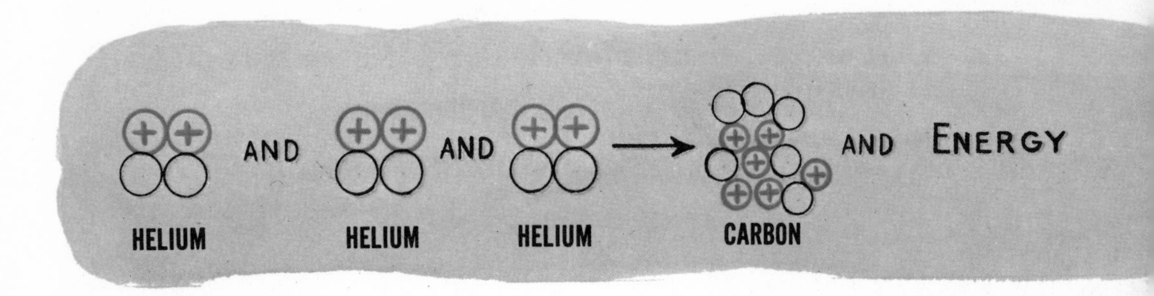


The Sun begins to expand again because of this new heat. Then it stops as the Sun runs out of helium. The Sun contracts again and heats again. It will keep on swelling and then getting smaller until the heavier elements like iron are being made in the nuclear reaction. But these heavier elements *do not* give any energy when they fuse. The Sun collapses violently, and the last nuclei that can fuse give out their energy in a big BANG, as the Sun finally explodes.

All that is left is a small, cool central bit, a tiny, quiet star -- a white dwarf.

## Things to Think About

1. What are sun spots? How do they affect us here on Earth?

2. How does the Sun get its energy? Explain the process.

3. How do the scientists know that the heat from the Sun does not come from burning coal or oil?

4. What do you suppose it would be like to orbit the Sun at a distance of about one million miles?

5. If you lived in another solar system, how would our Sun look to you?

6. What is meant by a magnetic field? What shape does a magnetic field have around a bar magnet? What shape does it have around a wire with an electric current? Experiment with iron filings and a magnet and a wire carrying a current from a dry cell to see this.

### What? Why? How?

You should never look directly at the Sun. However, you can use a telescope to project an image of the Sun onto a white screen, without looking at the Sun. Hold the telescope so the eyepiece is toward the screen and the telescope points directly at the Sun. You will be able to see the sunspots on the screen. (The image will be upside down.)

# EFFECTS OF THE SUN ON THE EARTH

All of us know that without the Sun, life on Earth would be impossible. It gives us light to see by and heat to keep us warm. However, the Sun does many things for us that we do not realize or think about.

The movement of Earth around the Sun and the position of the Earth in relation to the Sun cause the seasons on Earth. Why do we have seasons?

The fuel that we have to burn and the food we have to eat would be impossible without the Sun. How did the Sun furnish us with fuel? Exactly what does it do to furnish food?

When you listen to a weather report, you may hear the forecaster say "It will be a sunny day." The Sun has much more to do with our weather than just make it a sunny day, however. The Sun is a sort of giant air conditioner which operates all the time on our home, the Earth.

**What Causes Our Seasons?**

Do you know why the Earth has seasons? To understand the seasons, you must know that the imaginary line, or *axis*, on which Earth turns is tilted. The axis always tilts the same in its orbit around the Sun. Because the axis of the Earth is tilted, the Sun gives more heat to some parts of Earth than it does to others. Why?

Try shining a flashlight straight down on a table top. Notice how much space receives light rays. Try shining the light so it slants more. Now how much area does the light shine on? Light rays shining straight down cover less area than slanting rays, so they give the area more heat. This should show you why slanting rays from the Sun furnish less heat to the Earth than rays which come from nearly overhead.

The diagram will help you understand why Earth's seasons are caused by the tilt of the Earth's axis. Let's follow what happens in the Northern Hemisphere. About December 22, the Earth is in a position in which the Northern Hemisphere tilts away from the Sun and so receives slanted rays. Therefore, the Northern Hemisphere is not receiving much heat. This is the shortest day of the year and the first day of winter. It is called *winter solstice.* Earth continues moving in a counterclockwise direction. The days keep getting longer until the Earth reaches its March 22 position. At that time, the Sun shines directly down on the Equator. The periods of daylight and darkness are equal. This is called the *spring equinox* and is the first day of spring.

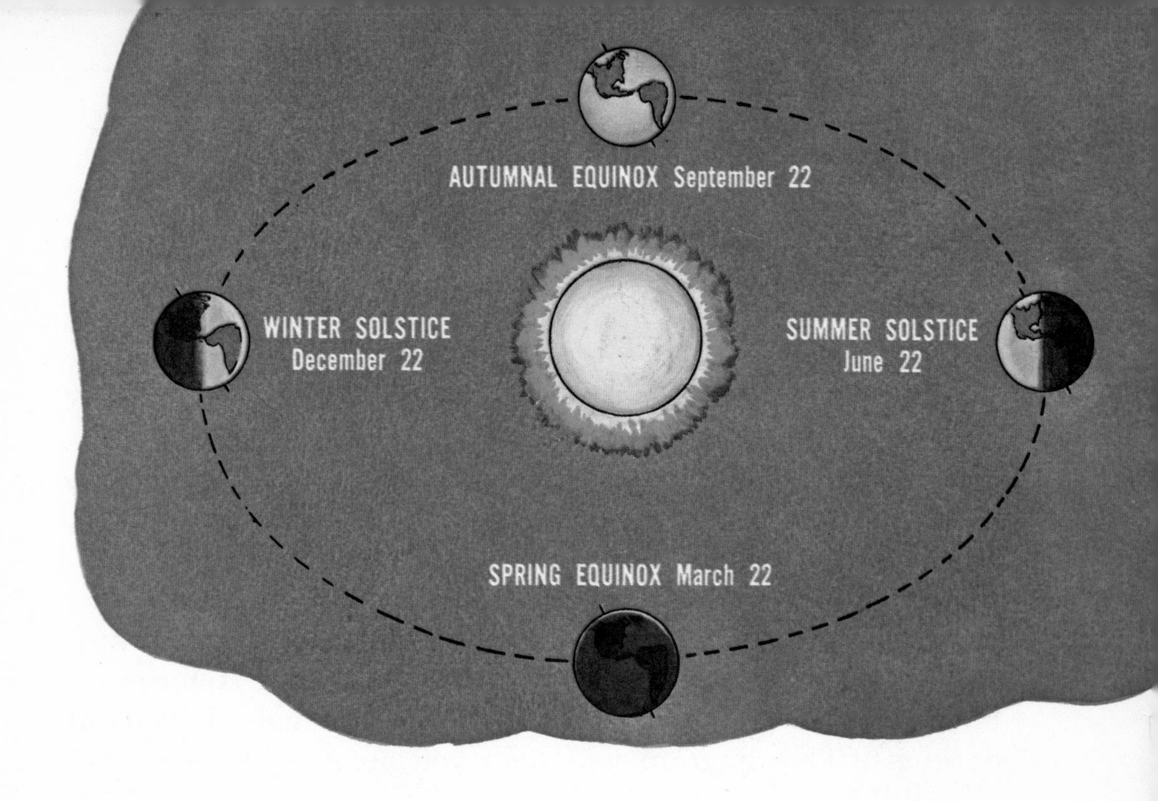


As the Earth continues in its orbit, the tilt of its axis is still the same, so now the Northern Hemisphere begins to tilt toward the Sun. By about June 22, the Earth has reached the position where the Sun is straight overhead as far north as it will ever be. This marks the first day of summer and is called the *summer solstice.* Then the Northern Hemisphere has the longest period of daylight of the whole year. As the Earth moves on, the daylight hours begin to get shorter again. By September 22, daylight and dark have become equal. This is the *autumnal equinox*. It is the first day of fall. As the Earth continues in its orbit, the daylight hours keep getting shorter and shorter in the Northern Hemisphere until it gets back to the shortest day about December 22.

When the Northern Hemisphere is getting Sun's rays that are slanted, the Southern Hemisphere is tilted toward the Sun and it is getting the rays from higher overhead. This makes the seasons in the Southern Hemisphere just the opposite of those in the Northern Hemisphere.

**Why Is There Day and Night?**

Day and night are caused by the rotation of the Earth. A day is 24 hours long because it takes 24 hours for the Earth to rotate once. The half of the Earth facing the Sun is always lighted and the other half is in darkness. If the axis of the Earth were not tilted, every spot on Earth would have periods of daylight and darkness 12 hours long. Actually, since the Earth is tilted on its axis, this happens only two days a year -- the first day of autumn and the first day of spring. When the Northern Hemisphere is tilted toward the Sun, more of the Northern Hemisphere is in the daylight for a longer time. Days are longer and the North Pole has 24 hours of daylight. At the same time, places in the Southern Hemisphere are having shorter days and the South Pole has 24 hours of darkness. The diagram will help you see why this is true.

As the Earth turns so your home nears the lighted side of the Earth, the Sun seems to come up over the horizon in the east. Your home keeps turning toward the Sun until, at noon, the Sun is the highest in the sky that it will be that day. During the afternoon, your home turns away until the Sun disappears from view because where you live is now on the dark side of the Earth.

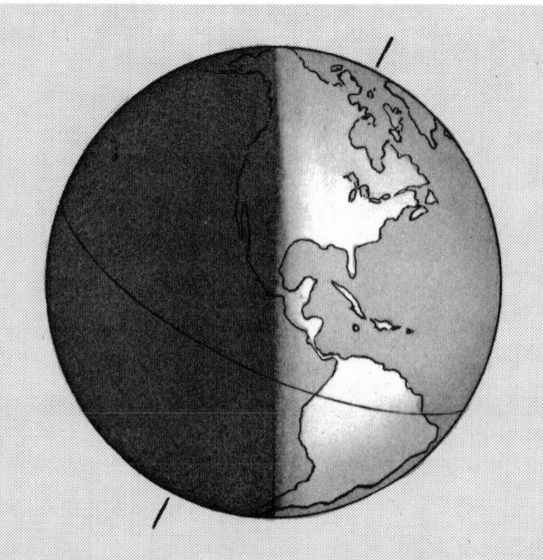

### How Does Earth Travel Around the Sun?

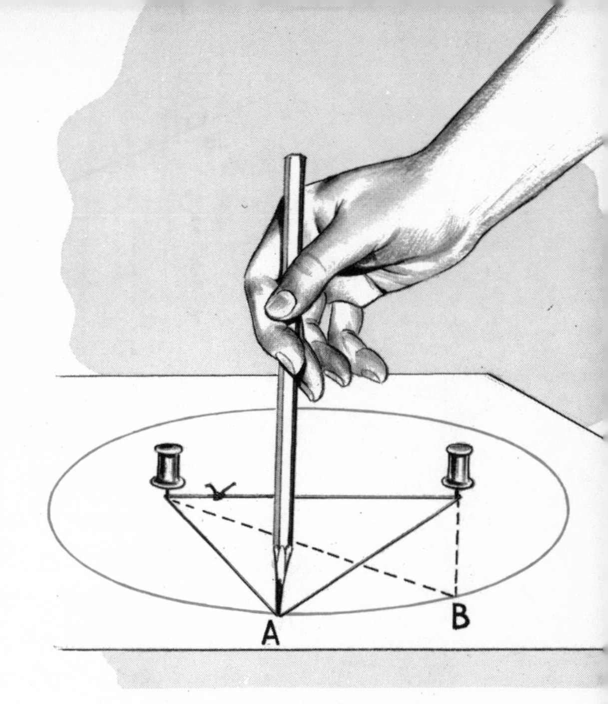


Earth does not travel around the Sun in a perfect circle. Its orbit is an *ellipse*. It looks something like a circle but is really oval-shaped.

You can draw one by using two small nails, a string, and a pencil. The point where a nail is located is called a *focus*. The Earth travels around the Sun in an elliptical orbit with the Sun at one focus and nothing at the other. If you draw an ellipse with the nails about 1/8 of an inch apart, the ellipse will be about the shape of the Earth's orbit.

You can see that a planet's distance from the Sun keeps changing. When a planet is closest to the Sun, it is said to be at *perihelion*. When it is furthest from the Sun, it is at *aphelion*. The Earth's perihelion distance is 91,500,000 miles. The aphelion distance is 94,500,000. Why do we say that the Earth is about 93,000,000 miles from the Sun?

It is important to understand that distance to the Sun has nothing to do with winter and summer. The seasons are due to the slant of the Sun's rays and the different slanting rays are due to the tilt of the Earth's axis.

### Will Earth's Axis Always Point to the North Star?

We have said that Earth's axis always keeps the same slant into space. This is not quite true. The axis keeps tilting just a little more as the years pass. After thousands of years, this will add up to quite a lot.

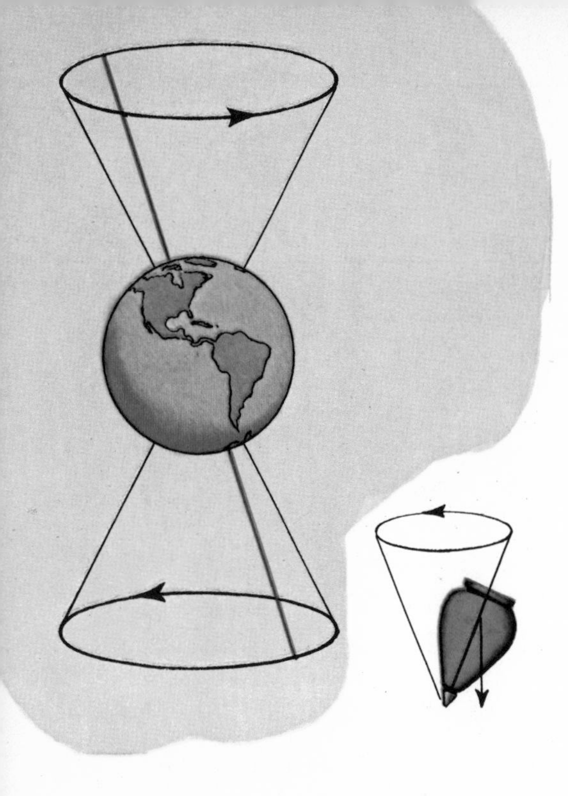

This diagram shows the axis as it is now. The axis traces a double cone in space. It takes 26,000 years for it to make a full revolution and get back to its original slant. This does not change the seasons during any one year. Yet after hundreds of years, Earth will tilt at a different angle, the Sun's rays will strike Earth differently, and the seasons will change. Then the axis will not be pointing toward the North Star.

This action of the Earth is called *precession*. It is much like what happens when a top spins, except that a top precesses rapidly. Earth's gravity pulls on the top's axis and it tips. Any point on the axis makes a circle as it goes around. The same kind of thing happens to the Earth. The force of gravity that pulls at the Earth is due to the Sun and Moon.

### How Does the Sun Furnish Food for Us?

While the Earth is traveling around the Sun, its day side receives energy in the form of sunlight. The sunlight warms Earth and the living things on it. If Earth did not get sunlight, we would have no food to eat. Energy from the Sun is used by green plants to manufacture food from carbon, hydrogen, and oxygen, by a process called *photosynthesis*. Water which plants get from the soil furnishes hydrogen and oxygen. A molecule of water contains two atoms of hydrogen and one atom of oxygen ($H_2O$). Carbon comes from carbon dioxide that plants get from the air. A carbon dioxide molecule contains one atom of carbon and two atoms of oxygen ($CO_2$).

With the help of a substance called *chlorophyll*, which is found in green plants, the energy of the Sun breaks apart the atoms in water and carbon dioxide and arranges them in a different way. It is a very complicated process but the end result is that sugars are manufactured by the plant, and oxygen is given off.

One of the simple sugars made by plants is *dextrose*. Its formula is $C_6H_{12}O_6$. You can see that molecules of water and molecules of carbon dioxide have the necessary molecules to produce simple sugar and oxygen. The sugar is a high energy food that can be used by your body. All other foods come indirectly from sugar.

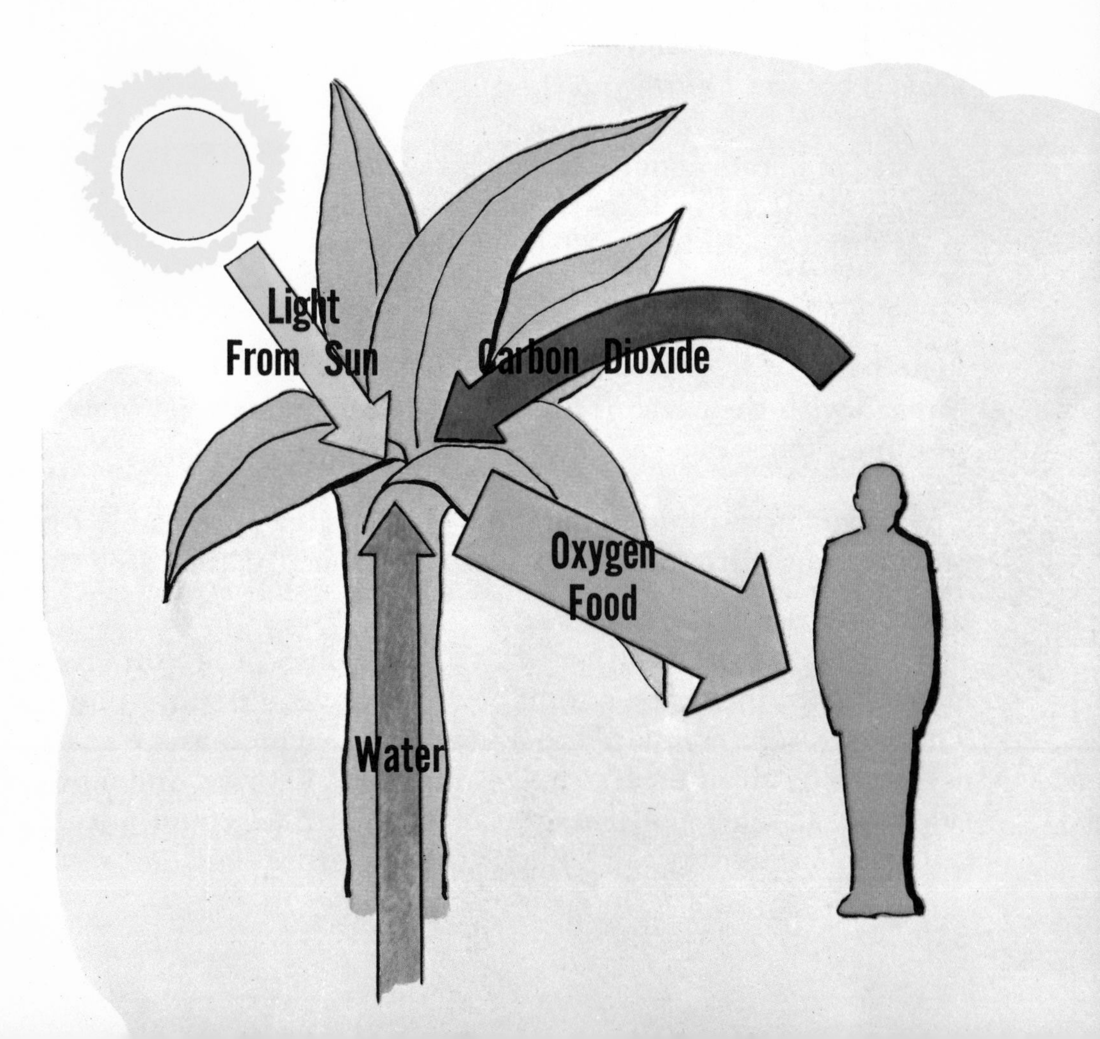

**How Is the Sun Responsible for Fuel?**

If you burn wood, which is really plant tissue, you can easily see that the fuel is almost directly from the Sun. But what about coal and petroleum which are very common fuels?

About 300 million years ago, a very favorable growing period started. It lasted for about 100 million years. During that time, plants grew very large and thick. What happened to them? The land became swampy, and the plants began to decay. Most of the hydrogen and oxygen in the plants escaped when they decayed. What was left was almost pure carbon. This kind of carbon material is called *peat* and can be used for fuel. As the ages passed, the peat was changed by heat and by great pressure due to continuous piling on of layer upon layer of sand and soil. The pressure and heat squeezed the moisture out of the peat. It became *lignite* and then coal.

A bed of plants about 100 feet thick was squeezed into a layer of coal about 7 feet thick. What made the plants possible? A great shining sphere, 93,000,000 miles away.

Petroleum, too, was formed from plants which were acted upon by great heat and pressure. However, hydrogen was also trapped with the carbon. From petroleum, we now get fuels -- gasoline, kerosene, gas, and oil -- all because of the Sun.

You can now understand how the Sun is responsible for providing us with fuels and foods for warmth and growth.

**How Does the Sun Affect the Weather?**

What makes the weather? In the first place, the Sun gives out energy, shines upon our planet, and moves our atmosphere. The Sun can be compared to a heat engine which uses our air as a working substance. It makes air warm up, rise, and move sideways. It takes moisture out of lakes and seas and puts it into the circulating air. Later the moisture falls as rain.

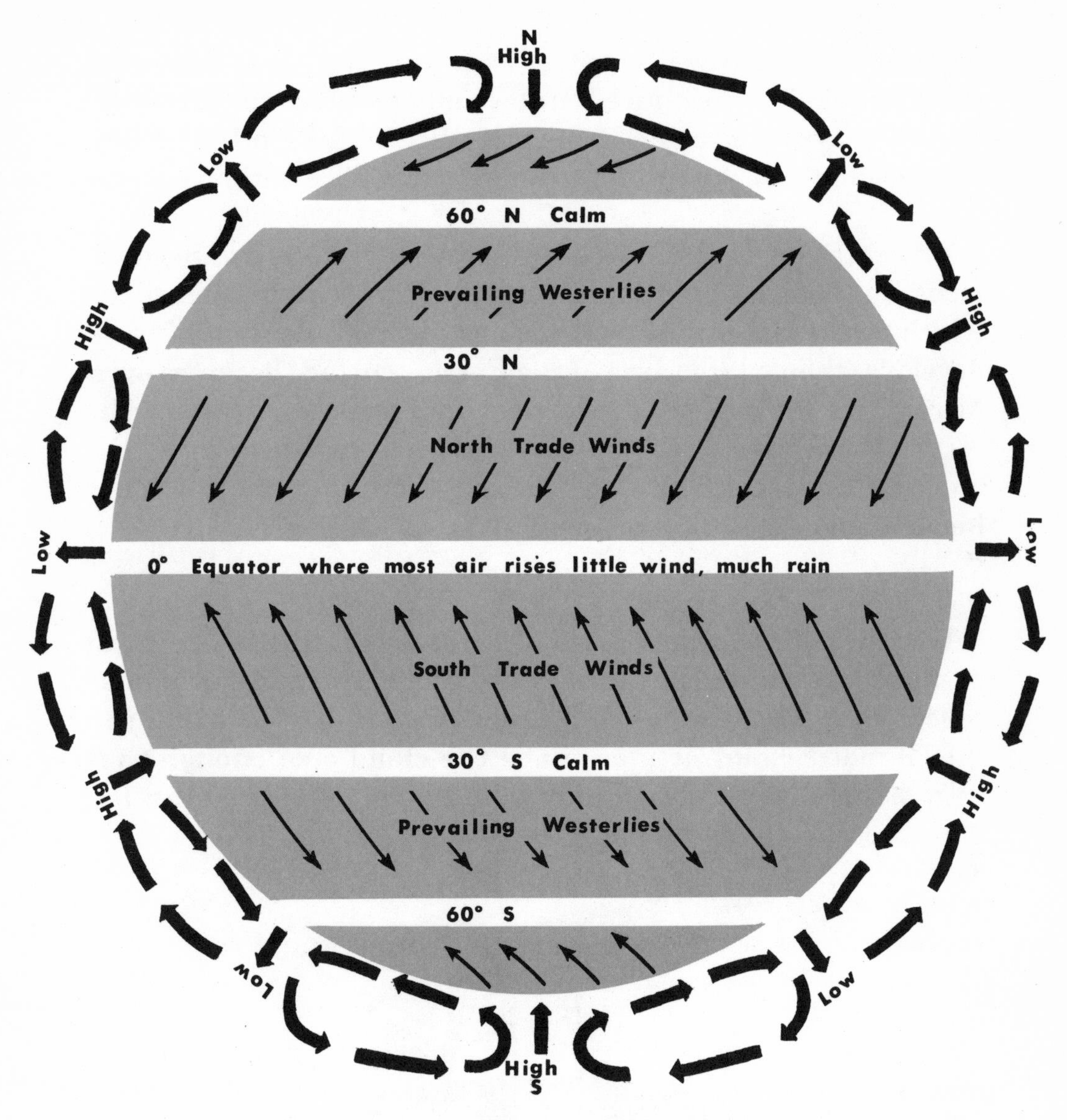


What else helps make the weather? The atmosphere surrounding a planet is very important. A thick atmosphere becomes heated and so holds heat near the Earth even at night when the Sun is not shining. The rotation of the Earth also affects the weather. By turning on its axis, Earth sends masses of air spinning in certain directions making large wind patterns over the surface of the Earth.

One of the large wind patterns is the *prevailing westerlies* which we find in the United States and any place east and west of it. The weather comes from the west in the United States. There is nothing we can do to change the large wind patterns.

The rotation of the Earth also sets up certain smaller patterns, the turning *highs* and *lows*. These are carried across the Earth by the larger air flows, such as the westerly winds. A low develops when a large area of the Earth's surface becomes overheated. The overheated air rises and escapes, leaving the region with less air. If the rising air has moisture in it, the moisture will condense as the air gets to cooler, greater heights, and it will rain or snow.

### How Can Weather Be Changed?

We can change small parts of these areas a little bit. Rain or snow falls when the air becomes cooler and cannot hold as much water vapor as when it was warm. If dry ice is dumped into a moist cloud, it may make the cloud cool enough that rain or snow will fall before it would have done so naturally. This process is called *seeding* the clouds.

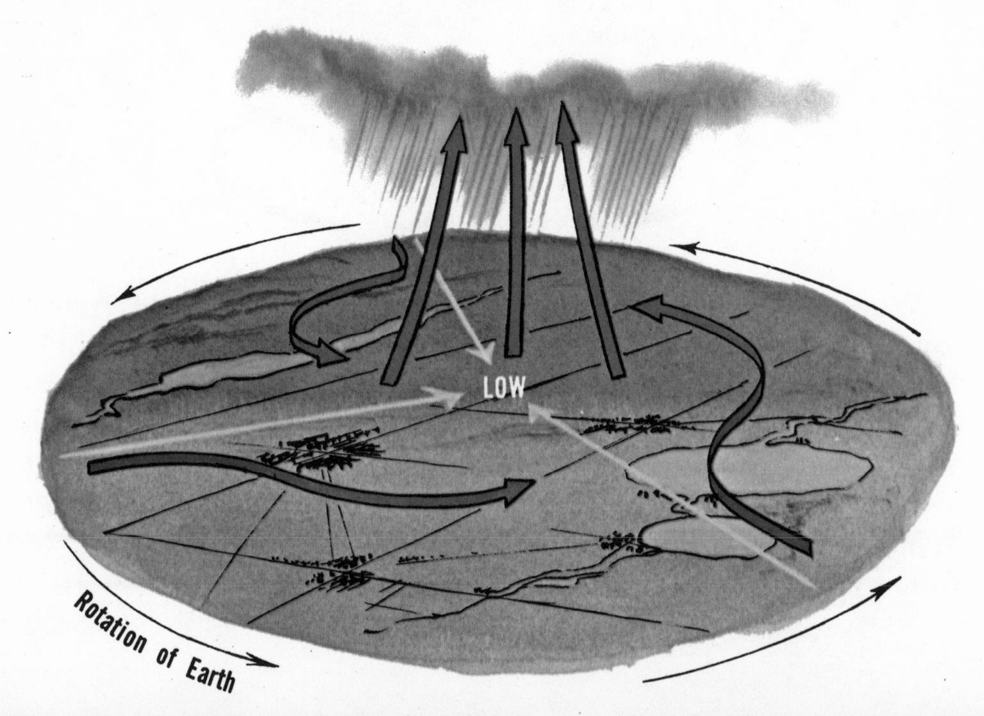

The United States has been sending up weather satellites, which are vehicles containing cameras that orbit Earth and take pictures of the weather. Weather satellites may also be used to seed clouds. They could release dry ice or chemicals far, far away and rain out a storm before it became dangerous. It may be possible too, for the chemicals to be dropped at just the right time to cause rain where it is especially needed. This is how it could be done.

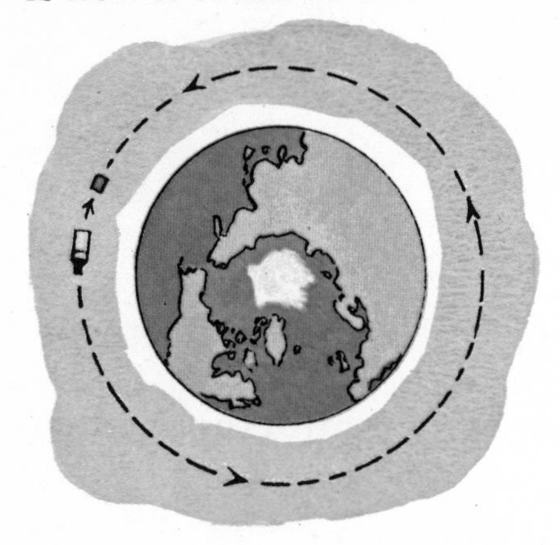

A can of chemicals to seed the clouds could be fired backward from the satellite and so lose some of its forward speed.

The can of chemicals would fall toward the atmosphere and clouds of a gathering storm.

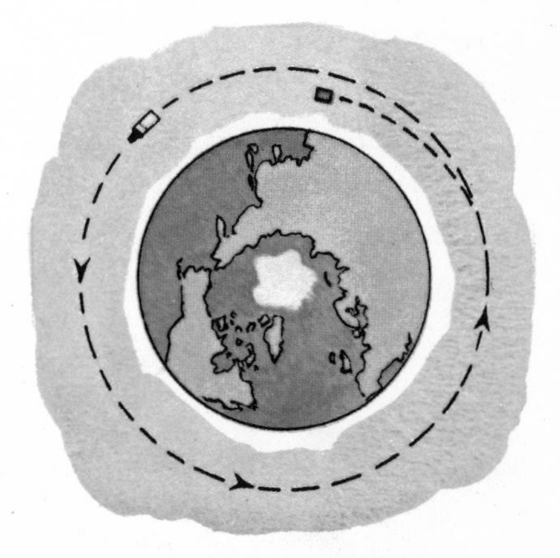

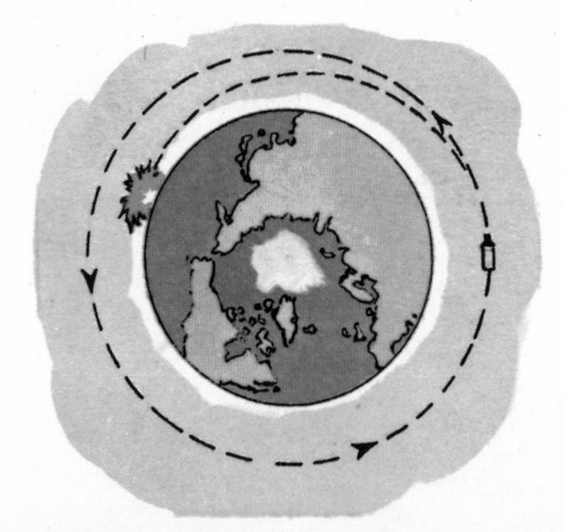

The can would break open as it entered the atmosphere and storm region, causing rain to fall and the storm to break up before it becomes violent.

## Things to Think About

1. What is the shape of the Earth's orbit around the Sun? How could you draw this figure?

2. How does the Sun cause our seasons?

3. What is precession?

4. If the Earth's axis were upright, would we have seasons?

5. Do you think it is a good idea to try to control the weather by using satellites?

6. How is the Sun responsible for us having food to eat?

7. Could there be a planet which has the same weather all the time?

**What?**

**Why?**

**How?**

See if the Sun is important to make plants grow. Take two of the same kind of plants. Plant them in flowerpots of the same size. Be sure both are good healthy plants. Put one in the window so it will get plenty of sunlight, put the other in a dark closet. Water them exactly the same amount. What happens to the two plants? How do you explain this?

# THE MOON--SATELLITE OF THE EARTH

A moon is any heavenly body which orbits a planet. Our Earth has only one moon, but several of the planets of our solar system have more than one. Moon sizes in our solar system vary from about 5 miles in diameter for one of the moons of Mars to over 3,000 miles in diameter for Europa, a moon belonging to Jupiter. Several moons are larger than ours. Ours is 2,160 miles in diameter and has about 1/80 as much mass as the Earth.

We usually say that a moon orbits its planet. The truth is that they orbit together. The Earth and Moon travel around the Sun together, while they are going around each other.

A few years ago we could only study the Moon through telescopes, but now we are learning more about it from spacecraft which have circled it and taken pictures, and from spacecraft which have landed there. Every day new things are being learned as a result of our space program.

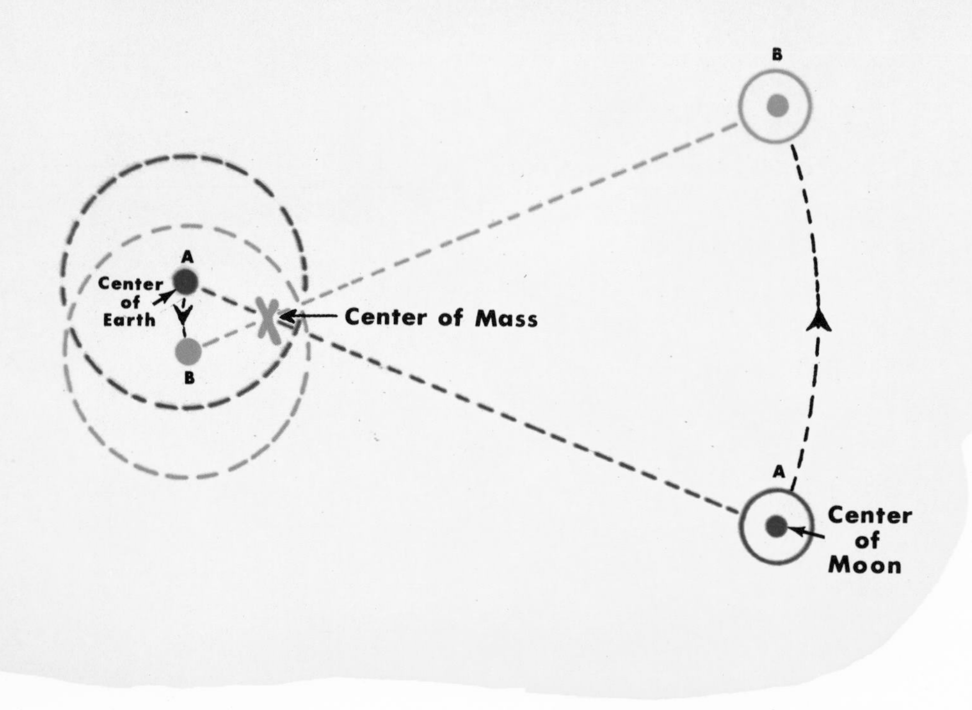


**How Do the Earth and Moon Orbit?**

The Earth and Moon orbit around each other just as though they were on the ends of a great seesaw. If you tried to seesaw with your father, you would need to have a much longer part of the plank so you would balance him. So it is with the Earth and Moon. The Earth is much larger than the Moon so it is closer to the *center of mass*, or what would be the balancing point. The diagram shows you how Earth and Moon move together as they are traveling around the Sun. The blue dots show the centers of the Earth and Moon in position *a*. When the center of the Earth has moved to position *b*, as shown by the red dot, the center of the Moon has moved to its position *b*. The Earth and Moon move with each other as if they were balls on the end of a rod and someone was twirling the rod.

The Moon goes around the Earth in an elliptical orbit. The closest point, its *perigee*, is about 219,000 miles. The furthest point, its *apogee*, is about 252,000 miles. We usually say that the Moon is about 240,000 miles away from us.

The Moon rotates once in about 27 days and 8 hours which is nearly the same length of time that it takes for it to orbit the Earth. That means that the same side of the Moon is always toward the Earth.

There is another interesting point between the Moon and Earth, and that is the point (on a line joining the two bodies) where the opposite pulls of gravity on a body are the same and so cancel each other. At this point, an object which happens to run out of speed at exactly that spot would be stuck there.

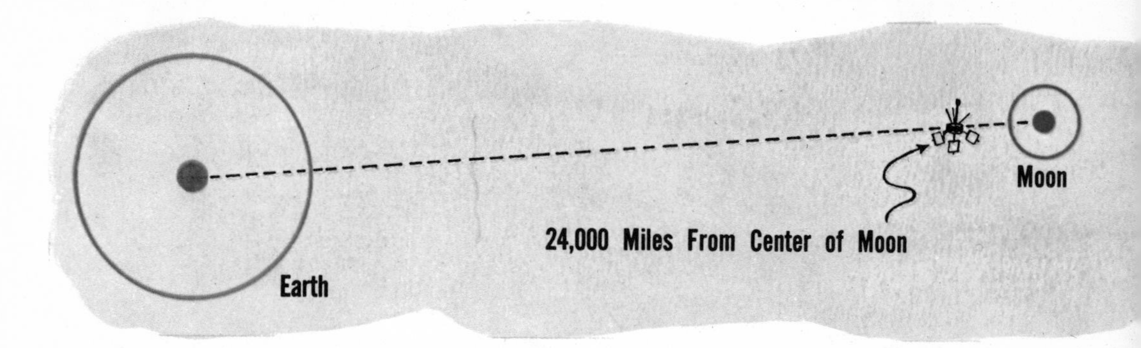


Two things really make this impossible, however. First, an object would always have a tiny bit of speed left,which would tend to carry it across the point, or it would lack a little speed and would fall back. Second, the Moon does not stand still so that this point keeps changing.

#### What Is the Gravity on the Moon?

Gravity on our Moon is about one-sixth as much as on Earth, so on the Moon, you would weigh only one-sixth of your Earth weight. Even a 300-pound Earthman would weigh only 50 pounds on the Moon. The strength of your muscles would be the same on the Moon. Think how easy it would be to do things. Think what a great athlete you would be. Imagine how far you could throw a ball, and how high you could jump.

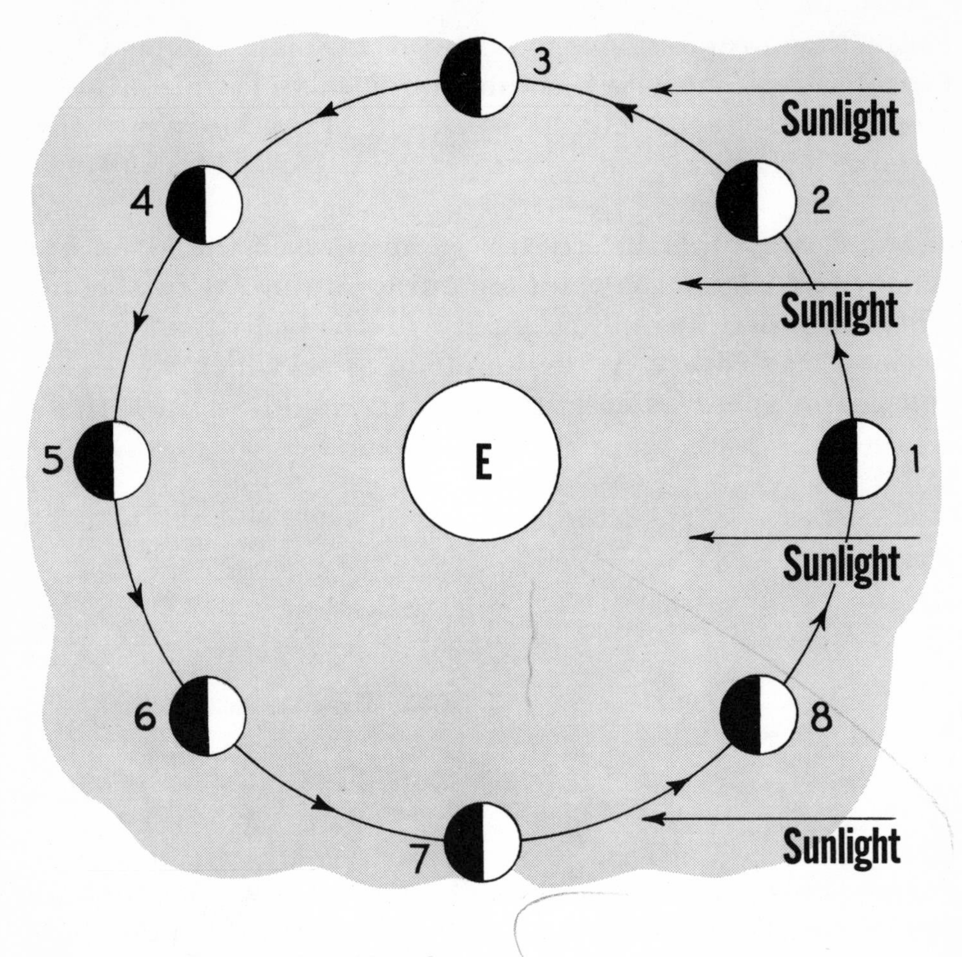


**What Are the Phases of the Moon?**

As the Moon travels around the Earth and they both travel around the Sun, the positions of the Moon, Earth, and Sun keep changing in relation to each other. The way we see the Moon from Earth keeps changing too. The Sun always lights the half of the Moon toward it, but we see all the lighted part only when we have a full moon. This occurs every 29 1/2 days. Because the shape of the Moon as we see it from Earth keeps changing, we say the Moon has *phases*.

The diagram will help you understand why we see the Moon differently here on Earth as it makes its trip around.

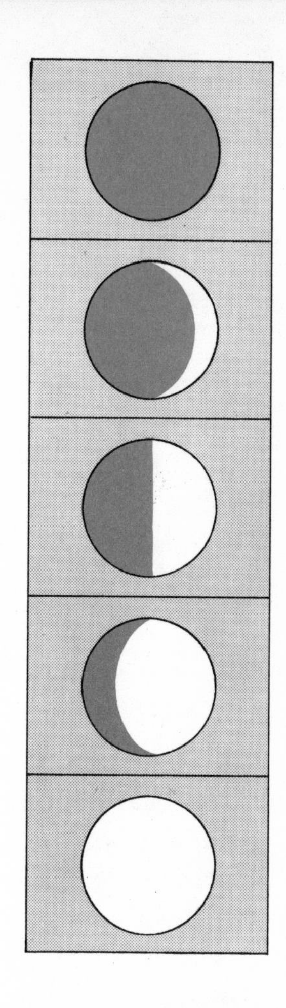

When the Moon is between the Earth and Sun, the lighted side is facing away from the Earth and we can see no light from it. This is a new moon.

The Moon moves counterclockwise and soon a crescent will be visible from Earth. During this time when the visible part of the Moon is getting larger, we say it is *waxing*.

When the Moon is one-fourth of the way around, it is called the first quarter. One-half of the lighted side can be seen.

Soon three-fourths of the lighted part can be seen. This is the phase called gibbous.

When the Moon is halfway around all the lighted part can be seen. This is the full moon.

The Moon starts the last half of its trip around Earth and part of the Moon begins to disappear. During this time when the visible part of the Moon is getting smaller, we say the Moon is *waning*.

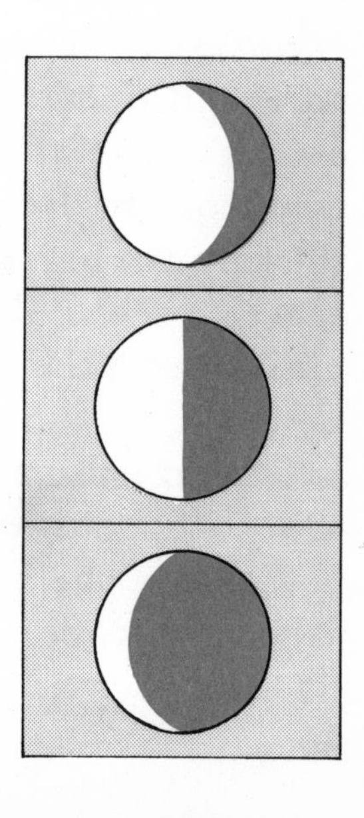

The Moon is soon in the gibbous phase, but this time, the three-fourths of the Moon on the opposite side is visible.

The Moon moves on to the last quarter and half of it is seen again but the opposite half from that seen the first quarter.

Finally only a crescent is seen, but the horns point in the opposite direction than before. Soon there will be a new moon again.

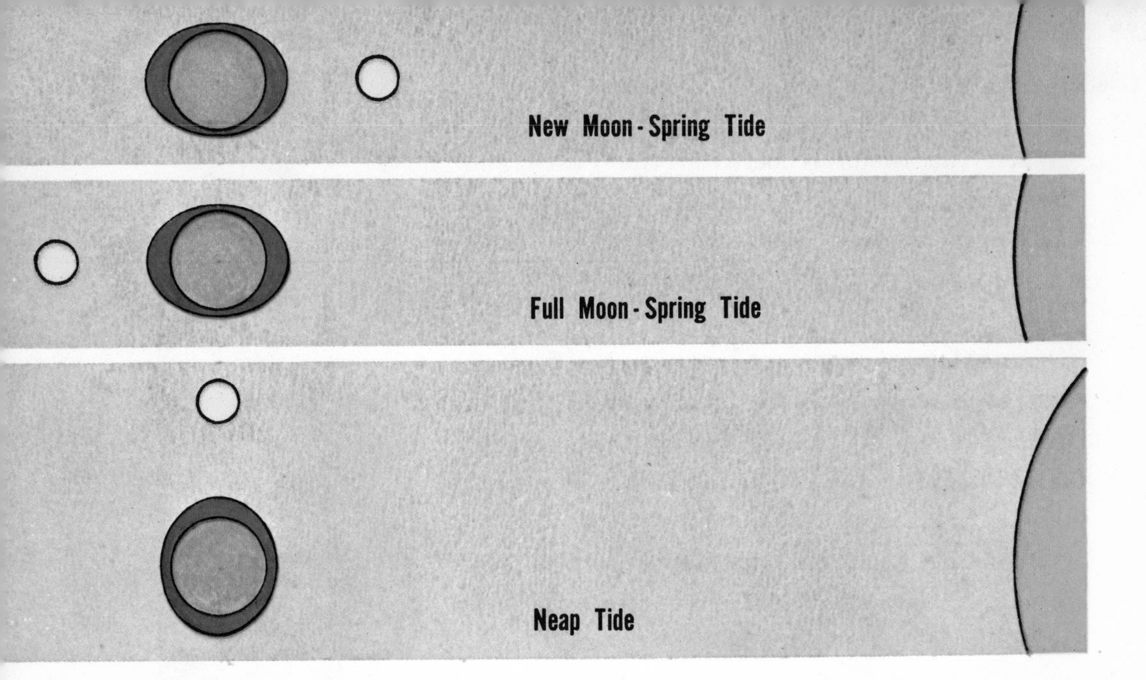


#### What Causes the Tides?

The regular rise and fall of ocean tides on Earth is due mostly to the pull of the Moon and partly to the pull of the Sun. There are two high tides daily, one when the Moon is high in the sky and the other when it is on the opposite side.

Since the ocean water is attracted by the pull of Moon's gravity, you might think that the water would rise on the moonlit side and fall on the opposite side. This is not true because the Earth can move freely in space. Therefore, its solid part is also attracted by the Moon and moves toward it. This causes the solid part of the Earth to be pulled away from the water on the far side. This makes the water deeper there, so the tide will be high. If you could look at a high tide from out in space, you would see a big bulge of water that seems to be running around the Earth.

The Sun also pulls on the water of Earth, but it is so far away that its effect is only about half that of the Moon. At full and new moon, the Sun and Moon help each other and cause very high tides, called *spring tides.*

At the first quarter and at the last quarter of the Moon, the Sun and Moon are working against each other so the high tides are not so high. These are called *neap tides.*

**Why Do We Have Eclipses?**

It is a strange fact of nature that the Moon seems to us here on Earth to be the same size as the Sun. Although the Sun is much larger, the Moon is so much closer that they appear to be about the same size. So if the Moon passes directly between the Earth and Sun, it can shut out the view of the Sun. When this happens, we have a *solar eclipse.*

Study the diagram and you will see that an eclipse is the shadow of the Moon as it falls on the Earth. Notice that one area on Earth is totally dark. That part of the shadow is called the *umbra.* If you were in that area when there was an eclipse, you would see a *total eclipse.* You could not see the Sun at all. There is another region of the Moon's shadow that is not quite so dark. It is called the *penumbra.* If you were in this area, only part of the Sun would be hidden, and you would see a *partial eclipse.*

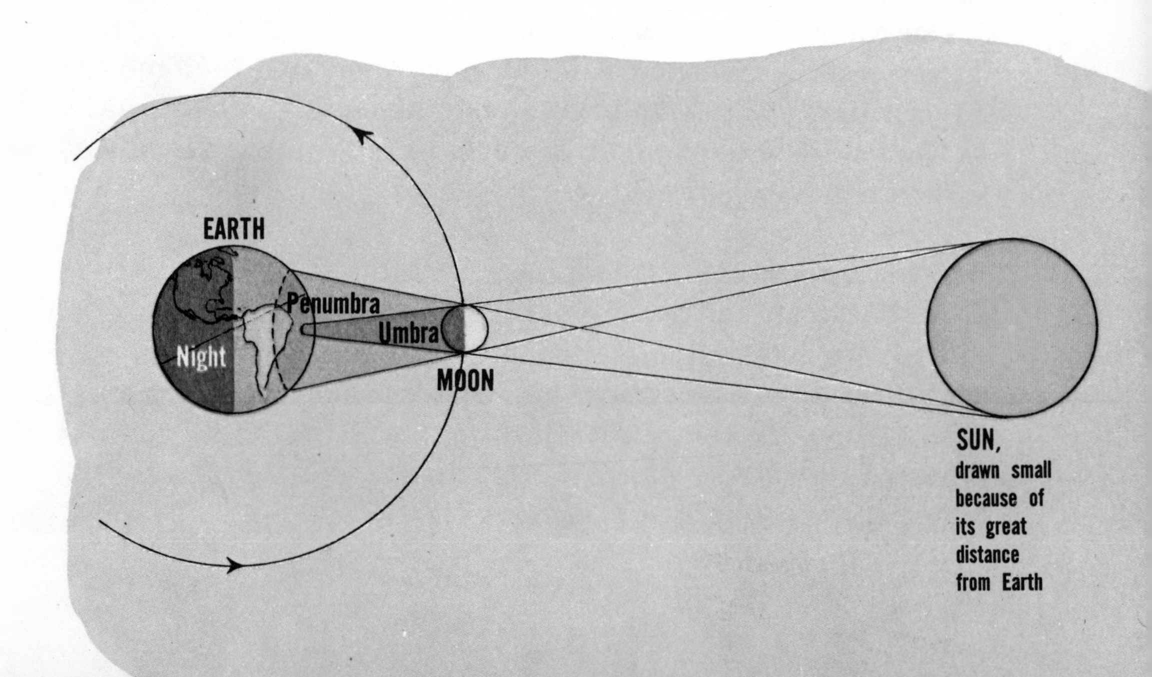

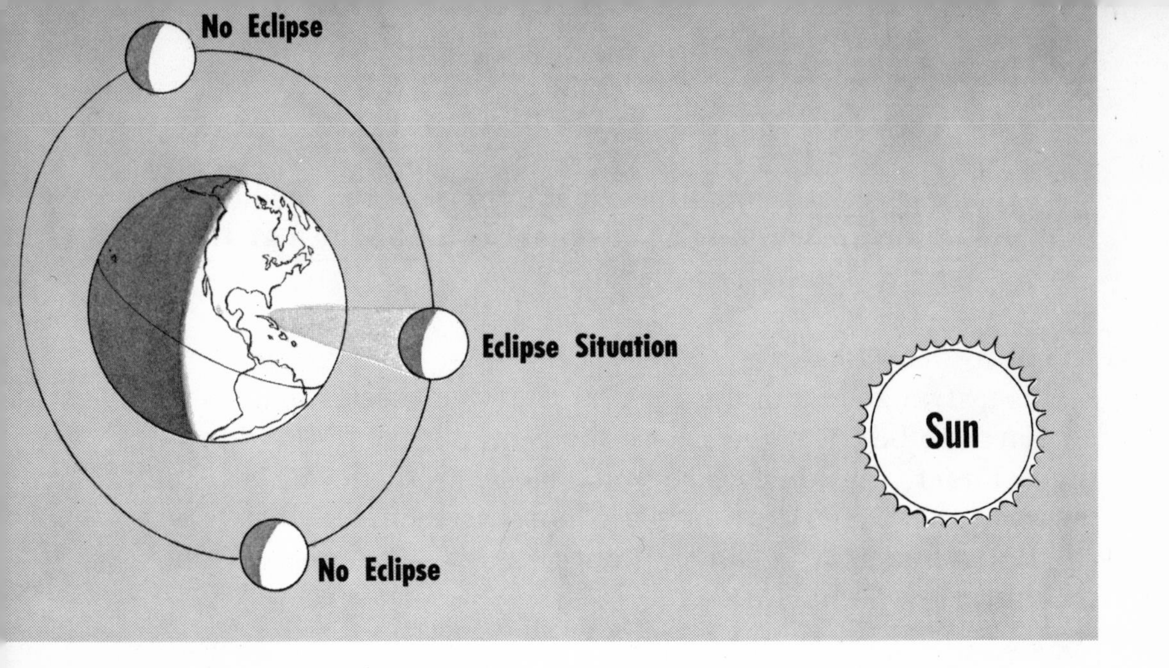


#### Why Don't We Have Eclipses More Often?

The three celestial bodies are not in a solar eclipse position every time the Moon is between the Sun and the Earth, or we would have an eclipse every month. For one thing, the Moon does not travel around the Earth in a circular orbit, but rather in an elliptical one. Therefore, its distance from Earth is not always the same.

The Moon does not orbit directly above the Earth's equator. This is another reason we do not have an eclipse each month. An eclipse is possible only when the Moon is above the equator of the Earth. Astronomers are able to tell many years ahead just when and where eclipses will occur.

#### What Can Be Learned From Eclipses?

Astronomers can learn much about the Sun by studying the spilled-over light, that is, the light which can be seen after the central bright photosphere has been blanked out by a total eclipse. Usually the Sun is so bright that the outer light is drowned out by it. When the blazing light is hidden by the Moon, the outer light appears very clearly.

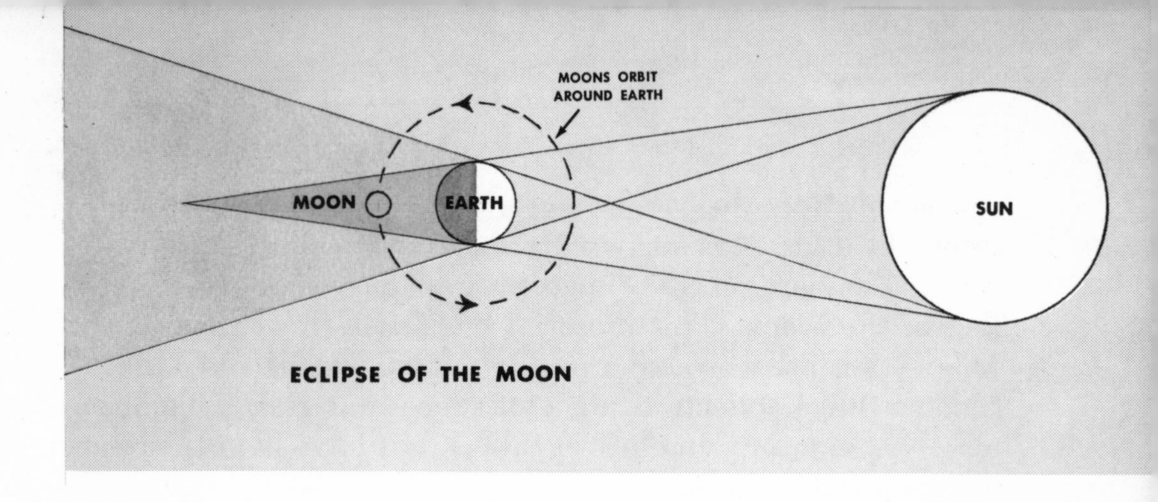

ECLIPSE OF THE MOON

**What Causes an Eclipse of the Moon?**

The Moon can be eclipsed, too. This is called a *lunar eclipse.* It happens when the Earth passes directly between the Sun and the Moon. The Earth gets into the path of the Sun's rays which would fall on the Moon, so the shadow of the Earth is cast on the Moon. An eclipse of the Moon can only occur at the position of the full moon when the Moon is on the side of the Earth away from the Sun.

**What Can Scientists Learn From the Moon?**

The Moon is one of the most interesting bodies of our solar system. It has no atmosphere, no water, no plants. Because of the lack of these, the Moon is very valuable to the world of science. For the very reason that the Moon is bare and has no atmosphere, it has remained unchanged since that time, billions of years ago, when the Sun and its family came into being. So, it will be wonderful to explore the Moon and see much of it as it was billions of years ago when it became solid.

We can find nothing here on Earth that shows how it looked when it all began. Winds, water, plants, animals, and chemicals have changed the Earth so completely that we can see no signs of the ancient days. The Moon, however, is our museum piece, saved for us by the extreme dryness and the vacuum around it.

Not only does the Moon have evidence about its own beginning, but it also has stray material from space, such as *meteorites*. They are pieces of meteors that have reached the surface of the Moon. This material has fallen by chance on the Moon's surface through the ages. It has made our shining Moon a huge collection place of space material. This space material may contain clues of things that have happened during the life of the solar system.

It is likely that the Moon has substances which have come from Earth itself. There may have been gigantic *eruptions* or explosions ages ago on Earth, and a few pieces of matter from the explosions may have reached our sky neighbor.

**What Will the Weather Be on the Moon?**

The temperatures on the Moon will not be comfortable for the astronauts who go there. It has no atmosphere to keep the temperature fairly even. The temperature may vary from 270 degrees F. during the lunar day to -270 degrees F. at night. Even moving from sunlight to shadow could mean a big difference in temperature.

Of course, the Moon has no rain or snow because there is no water there.

### Can There Be Life on the Moon?

Perhaps the Moon itself emerged from Earth during the time that the hot Earth was spinning on its axis and forming into a planet. If we find any signs of substances from Earth on the Moon, then the idea of *panspermia* will become an interesting study. Panspermia is the theory that life may spread from one body to another when *spores*, or tiny living things, make long journeys across the vast spaces that separate the planets and the moons.

The idea of panspermia was once believed by the great scientist, Svante Arrhenius, but few scientists believed the theory. In the first place, they wondered how the substances carrying spores could escape from a planet. Or, did these spores come as space travelers within their spaceships--the meteors? Or, did tiny living things come alone, pressed forward across space by the rays of a Sun? If this occurred, why didn't powerful ultraviolet rays of the sunlight destroy the tiny spores?

### Does the Moon Have Atmosphere?

It is said that the Moon has no atmosphere. However, this is not entirely true. There are traces of gases on the Moon. Some are because of radioactive decay of rocks. Some are due to volcano-like eruptions which occur on the Moon at times.

Scientists began to wonder. Is the Moon still hot inside? If it is, is it possible that there might be tiny forms of life below the surface? However, if simple life forms are on the Moon, they would not be capable of developing much because of the lack of water and atmosphere. Therefore, the Moon might be a museum of living things, too. It may show us how living things started millions of years ago.

We are studying the Moon because we want to know more about the *universe* which includes everything around us.

### What Is on the Surface of the Moon?

Spacecraft of Ranger, Lunar Orbiter, and Surveyor series have taken pictures of the surface of the Moon. Scientists now have so much knowledge of the Moon that they are able to make very complete maps of the surface. Even the side of the Moon never seen from Earth has been photographed.

Pictures of the Moon have shown that a large part of its surface is covered with holes, called *craters*. Some of these are quite large. Others are very small. Scientists do not agree about what has caused these craters. Most scientists now believe that most of the craters were formed by meteorites hitting the surface. However, there is evidence that some were formed by volcanic action.

One large crater is named Copernicus. It has several small craters around it. Scientists think they might be caused by small pieces of rock that were thrown out by a volcano which made the large crater. The crater also has white streaks which extend out from the crater like rays.

There are large flat areas on the Moon which can be seen as light-colored spots. These areas have been called seas by scientists, but really they are dry, flat plains.

There are also high mountains on the Moon. Scientists have measured their height by measuring the shadows they cast. They are found to be very high and very wide. Deep valleys called *rilles* run across the surface in some places. In other places there are ridges that look like wrinkles on the surface.

#### How Is the Moon Being Studied?

The first important studies of the Moon were probably made by Galileo many years ago. He made much better telescopes than had been made before, and he studied the surface of the Moon through these telescopes. He found that the surface was not smooth as the scientists of that time thought.

Our atmosphere keeps astronomers from getting a very clear view of celestial bodies. So when men were able to send up artificial satellites to orbit the Earth, they could get clearer pictures than ever before. Later spacecraft went to the Moon or around it and sent back pictures.

#### What Have Flying Cameras Revealed About the Moon?

A Russian spacecraft, Lunik 3, orbited the Moon and photographed about 70 percent of the side of the Moon that we cannot see from this planet. The camera was about 40,000 miles above the surface of the Moon at the time the pictures were taken.

United States scientists made many excellent pictures of the Moon by a series of flights by spacecraft called "Ranger." Ranger spacecraft were expected to crash on the Moon, but before they did they were to send back television pictures taken as they neared the Moon. This picture was taken by Ranger 7. It was taken 15 minutes and 6 seconds before Ranger 7 crashed. It was taken at an altitude of 1,063 miles and shows an area 260 miles wide. North is at the top of the picture. The crater seen at the right at the bottom is Arzachel. At center right is Alphonsus. The craters at the right are really rounder than shown because the camera took the picture at a low angle and because the Moon curves there.

**What Is Learned From Soft Landings on the Moon?**

After spacecraft had been made to crash on the Moon, the next step was to send spacecraft that would land softly. That is, they would land so gently that the spacecraft and cameras and other equipment would not be damaged. The first such spacecraft from the United States was Surveyor 1. It took over 11,000 pictures, many of them unusually clear. The cameras on Surveyor 1 were able to photograph individual rocks which were lying around. These rocks seem to have been hurled out of spots where meteorites have crashed into the Moon.

A number of Surveyor spacecraft were sent to the Moon to land at different spots in order to pick a good spot for the first landing of astronauts. Later Surveyors had devices to pick up soil and test it to see what was in it. Surveyor 5 tested the Moon's surface rocks and reported them to be like basalt rocks found on Earth. Rocks and soil that were tested contained these elements in about these amounts: oxygen (58 percent), silicon (18.5 percent), aluminum (6.5 percent), iron-nickel (5.5 percent), magnesium (3 percent), and a little carbon. The findings make the scientists believe even more strongly that Earth and Moon were formed from the same materials at the same time.

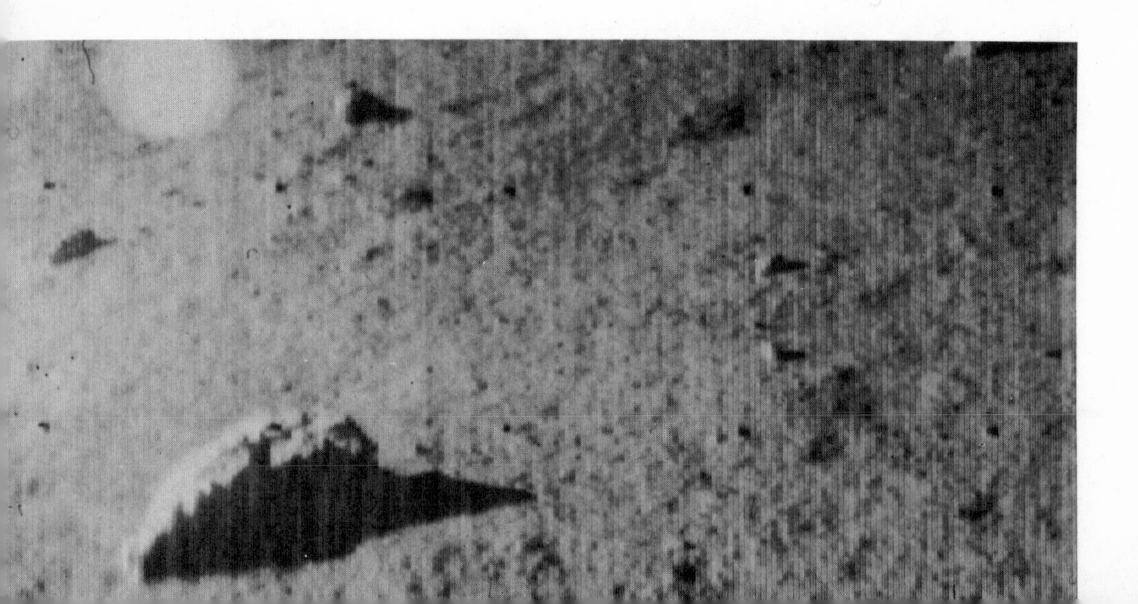

## Things to Think About

1. What are some of the ways the Moon affects the Earth?

2. What causes the phases of the Moon?

3. What is a spring tide? What causes it?

4. What causes an eclipse of the Sun? Why doesn't it happen more often?

5. Why do scientists want to study the surface of the Moon?

6. What is panspermia? Do you think it is possible?

7. What will be the biggest problems of people who live on the Moon for any length of time?

8. How does the Earth look from the Moon?

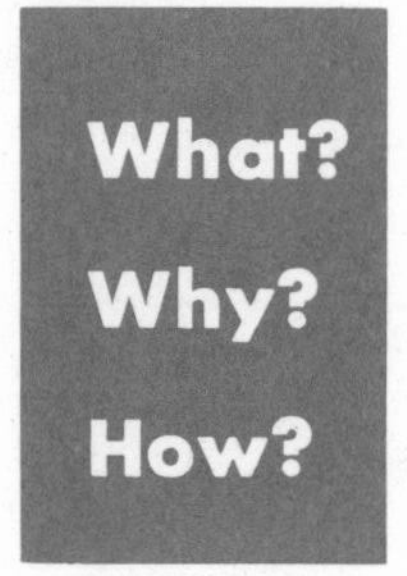


Things happen so fast in discoveries about space that books cannot keep up-to-date.

Read current science magazines and newspapers and see what is happening right now in the study of the Moon. What are the newest tools? What has been learned recently?

FIRST COLOR PHOTO OF EARTH TAKEN FROM SPACE

# FROM MERCURY TO PLUTO

The nine planets of the solar system are quite different in many ways. These differences are caused by the distance from the Sun, their size, and other factors.

Planets that are close to the Sun will have little or no atmosphere because it is blown away by the Sun's rays. Planets that have no atmosphere are very hot on the side toward the Sun and very cold on the side away from the Sun. It is the atmosphere that becomes heated and keeps all the heat from escaping into space. Even with atmosphere, planets far away from the Sun will be cold all the time because not enough heat from the Sun reaches them.

New ways are being developed to study the planets and new facts are being discovered. Astronomers are learning more and more, especially about the planets near the Earth. Some things scientists had believed have been proved wrong. Knowledge will continue to grow as our space program continues.

# Planets of the Solar System

| Planets | Average Distance From Sun (Millions of Miles) | Diameter (Miles) | Time of Rotation (Earth Time) | Time of Revolution (Earth Time) | Orbital Velocity (Miles per second) | Escape Velocity (Miles per second) |
|---|---|---|---|---|---|---|
| MERCURY | 36 | 3,000 | 59 days | 88 days | 29.8 | 2.2 |
| VENUS | 67 | 7,700 | 249 days | 225 days | 21.8 | 6.3 |
| EARTH | 93 | 7,900 | 24 hours | 365¼ days | 18.5 | 7.0 |
| MARS | 142 | 4,200 | 24 hr. 37 min. | 687 days | 15.0 | 3.1 |
| JUPITER | 483 | 86,700 | 9 hr. 55 min. | 12 years | 8.1 | 37.0 |
| SATURN | 886 | 71,500 | 10 hr. 14 min. | 29½ years | 6.0 | 22.0 |
| URANUS | 1783 | 30,000 | 10 hr. 40 min. | 84 years | 4.2 | 13.0 |
| NEPTUNE | 2783 | 28,000 | 15 hr. 40 min. | 165 years | 3.4 | 14.0 |
| PLUTO | 3675 | 6,500(?) | 7 days (?) | 248½ years | 2.9 | 6.6 (?) |

| Planets | Density (lbs. per cubic foot) | Weight of Human (100 lbs. on earth) | Number of Moons | Diameter of Moons (Miles) | Distance to Moons (Thousands of Miles) |
|---|---|---|---|---|---|
| MERCURY | 178.46 | 38 | 0 | — | — |
| VENUS | 303.26 | 88 | 0 | — | — |
| EARTH | 344.45 | 100 | 1 | 2,160 | 240 |
| MARS | 247.10 | 39 | 2 | 3 to 5 | 6 to 15 |
| JUPITER | 83.62 | 240 | 12 | 15 to 3,200 | 112 to 14,800 |
| SATURN | 44.30 | 117 | 10 | 300 to 3,500 | 115 to 8,100 |
| URANUS | 79.25 | 105 | 5 | 150 to 1,000 | 80 to 360 |
| NEPTUNE | 98.59 | 141 | 2 | 200 to 2,300 | 220 to 5,000 |
| PLUTO | 330.72 | 65(?) | 0 | — | — |

### What Can You Learn From the Tables?

The tables on the two pages you have just read will give you much information about the planets. They can be used to show how the planets are alike and different.

The distance of each planet from the Sun must be an average figure. You remember that the planets have an aphelion and a perihelion. The number given as the distance from the Sun is an in-between number.

Some of the measurements given are just guesses because it has been impossible to measure accurately in some cases. Facts about Pluto are not very accurate because it is too far away. For instance, scientists think Pluto has no moons, but they realize when better telescopes come into use and when the telescopes can be set up on space stations above the atmosphere, they may find that Pluto does have one or more moons.

The period of revolution for each planet is the length of time it takes to go around the Sun as measured by Earth time. Of course, these periods of time are quite different. Why are they so different? Does each planet move at the same speed? Does each one have the same distance to go?

Some measurements may change as the scientists discover new facts. One example of this is the rotation time of Mercury. Until recently, it was believed that the period of rotation and the time for one revolution were the same. Astronomers have now discovered that the period of rotation is about 59 days instead of 88 as they had believed.

What do you notice about the speed at which each planet moves in its orbit? Which planet moves the fastest? Which is slowest? What pattern do you notice? Why do you think this is true?

**What Is Escape Velocity?**

The velocity of escape from each planet is shown in miles per second. Do you know what *escape velocity* means? It means the slowest speed at which we must shoot some object to make sure that it will overcome the planet's gravity and escape completely, never to fall back on the planet. Remember, this is to be a one-shot performance, not simply a lift-off with the continuing burning of fuel, far, far into space. Do you see the difference? If you are willing to continue firing (which means using up more and more fuel), then you can escape at 50 miles per hour if you continue to burn fuel and more fuel and more fuel. Escape velocity is really the speed which will tear an object completely away from a planet and allow it to sail away into space without any need of burning more fuel. As you can see, escape velocity from Earth is 7 miles per second. Can you change miles per second to miles per hour? How much is this in miles per hour?

Would it be easy to escape from Jupiter? The escape velocity is 37 miles per second, which is 133,200 miles per hour. It would be very difficult for a spaceship to escape from there. On the other hand, it would take a speed of only 7,920 miles per hour to escape from Mercury.

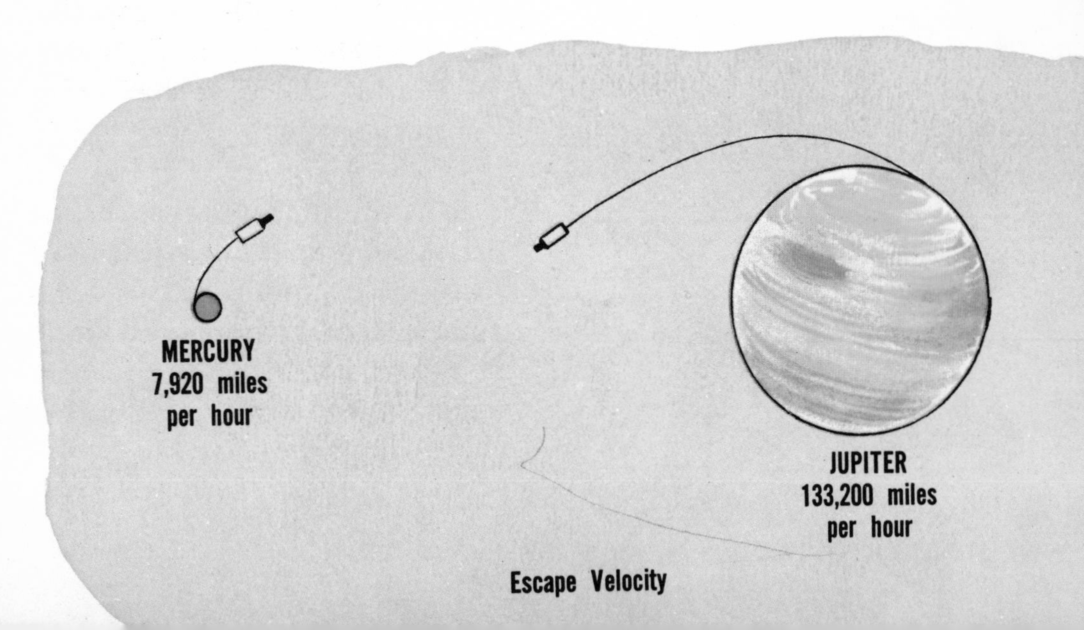


Escape Velocity

### Would Time Be Different on Mars?

One column tells the length of day for each planet. Notice that for Mars, the length of day, according to Earth time, is 24 hours, 37 minutes. This means that people from Earth visiting Mars will feel a natural day and night rhythm which is only 37 Earth minutes longer than Earth time. The time for going to bed at night, getting up in the morning, and eating meals would not seem strange to you.

If you should wear a wristwatch on Mars, would it run at exactly the same rate as here on Earth? Would a pendulum clock on Mars keep exactly the same time as one on Earth? The answer to the first question is "yes" and to the second one "no." Why do you think this is true?

You can understand if you know what makes each of them run. The wristwatch runs because a spring in the watch has been coiled tightly, and as it unwinds slowly, it moves the hands of the watch. The action would be the same anywhere in the universe. The speed with which the spring unwinds is not affected by the size of the planet or the amount of gravity. It would be just the same out in space.

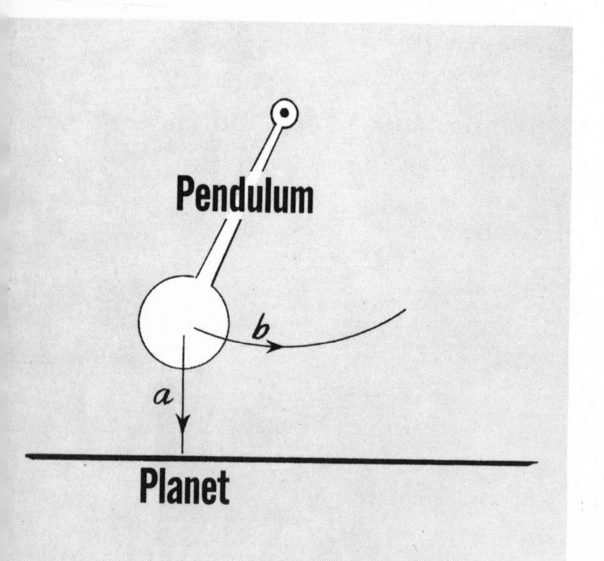


A pendulum, however, beats because a planet's gravitational force is pulling on the bob. Therefore, the stronger the pull of gravity, the faster the bob would swing, and the faster the clock would run.

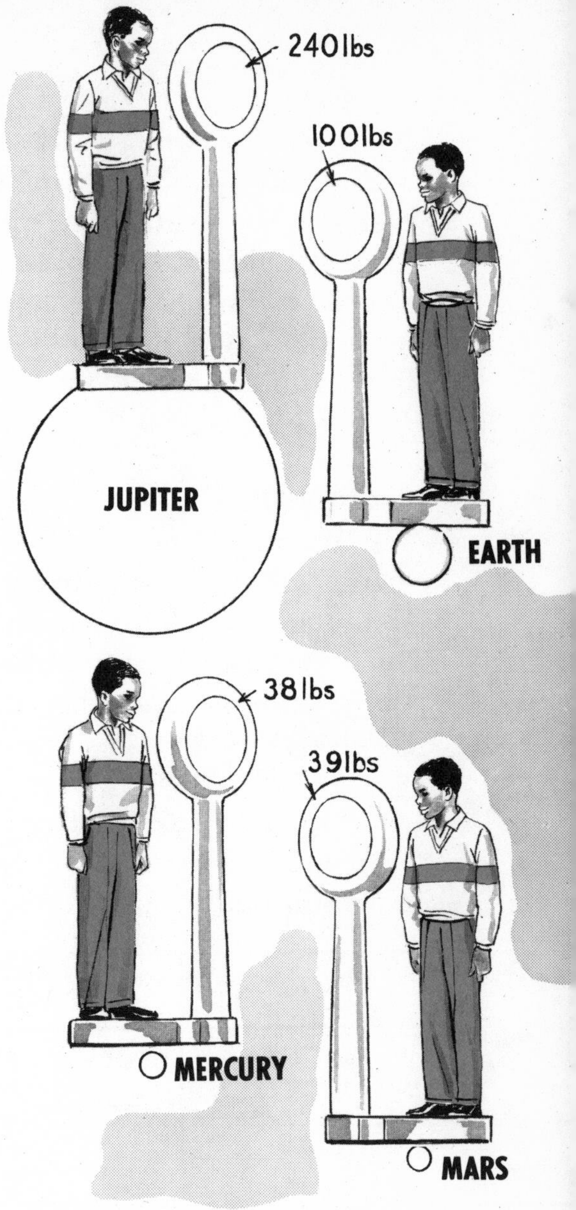

### How Dense Is Material in the Planets?

One part of the table tells the average density of each of the planets or the amount of mass it has. When the Sun was discussed, its density was compared to the density of water. The density of water was said to be 62.4 pounds a cubic foot. The density of the planets is also compared to the density of water. The average density of the Earth is over 5 1/2 times that of water. Notice that the density of the two largest planets is much less than that of the smaller ones. Jupiter has a density only slightly more than the density of water. Saturn is less dense.

### How Much Is the Pull of Gravity on the Planets?

The total amount of mass that a planet contains affects the force with which gravity would pull on an object on the surface of the planet. If you weighed 100 pounds on Earth, you would weigh only 38 pounds on Mercury. But imagine how hard it would be for you to jump or even walk on Jupiter. You would weigh 265 pounds. On the other hand, a Martian moon is so small and would have such a slight pull of gravity that you would weigh only about an ounce on it.

240 lbs
100 lbs
JUPITER
EARTH
38 lbs
39 lbs
MERCURY
MARS

### How Many Moons Are in the Solar System?

You can see from the information on the chart that the nine planets have a total of 32 moons. The small planets of Mercury, Venus, and Pluto do not have any. Actually, if Pluto had small moons, we would not be able to see them with telescopes. The large planets of Jupiter and Saturn have the most moons. In fact, Jupiter has a moon which is larger than the planet Mercury.

### What Are Future Plans for the Space Program?

Plans are already being made for travel to other planets. What will the space travelers find when they arrive there? What temperature will it be? Will there be atmosphere? Scientists have been able to make some measurements of these things. This chart shows what the scientists have discovered thus far.

Which of the planets do you think we might send spacecraft to first? Distance to the planet must be considered as well as conditions on the planet.

| PLANET | TEMPERATURE (Average) | ATMOSPHERE |
|---|---|---|
| MERCURY | 650 degrees F on sunlit side to about —400 degrees on hidden side | Practically vacuum |
| VENUS | 30 degrees at top of clouds to 500 degrees at surface | Carbon dioxide, nitrogen, water vapor |
| EARTH | About 60 degrees | Nitrogen, oxygen, water vapor, carbon dioxide, and small quantities of other gases |
| MARS | 80 degrees, day, to —150 degrees, night | Carbon dioxide, traces of water vapor, nitrogen, argon |
| JUPITER | About —200 degrees | All have hydrogen, helium, ammonia, methane, nitrogen gases, and these same elements in liquid and frozen form |
| SATURN | About —250 degrees | |
| URANUS | About —350 degrees | |
| NEPTUNE | About —370 degrees | |
| PLUTO | About —400 degrees | |

Venus

### What Are Conditions on Mercury?

Mercury has no atmosphere, no water, no plants. It is much like our Moon, but larger. The temperature on the side of Mercury facing the Sun at any time might be 600 to 700 degrees F. At the same time, the other side may be much below zero. This is because there is no atmosphere which is warmed on the sunny side and then circulates to the dark side and warms it.

### What Are Conditions on Venus?

Venus is the planet closest to Earth, but one about which we knew very little until recently. The surface is covered with thick clouds which keep it hidden from astronomers with telescopes. It was even difficult to measure the size of the planet accurately, because the height of the clouds was not known. New radio telescopes which measure by using radio waves, helped scientists learn more about Venus. Then United States launched Mariner 2 and later Mariner 5 spacecraft which flew by. The instruments on the spacecraft took measurements of the flyby.

The Russians landed the first unmanned spaceship, or space vehicle, on the surface of Venus. The Russian spacecraft, Venus 4, weighed 842 lbs. It left a larger capsule at a height of 15 1/2 miles above the surface of Venus. At that height, the temperature was recorded at 104 degrees F, but 1 hour and a half later, when the vehicle had been lowered by a parachute close to the surface, the temperature was 536 degrees F. At 15 1/2 miles above the surface, the pressure of the atmosphere was found to be about like that on Earth. Near the surface, it measured about 22 times as great. This atmosphere was found to be about 98 percent carbon dioxide, 1.6 percent water, and .4 percent oxygen. However, the U.S. Mariner 5, which flew past after Venus 4,found that the percentage of carbon dioxide was 72 to 87 percent. Both spacecraft reported a thin crown of hydrogen gas on the outer edge of the atmosphere. The Russian vehicle did not detect any magnetic field, but Mariner 5 did find a weak magnetic field.

It is hard to believe that there could be life on Venus -- the kind of life we know on Earth. Maybe high in the clouds where it is not so hot, there might be some living things, like bacteria, and even larger, floating forms. Maybe some could exist in the ground below the very hot surface.

Since the surface cannot be seen with optical telescopes, astronomers could not tell how the planet rotated. Recent studies show that Venus turns in the opposite direction from that which it takes around the sun. All the other planets rotate the same direction in which they revolve.

Venus has phases just like the Moon because its orbit between the Earth and the Sun causes its lighted portion to show up differently here on Earth.

**What Are the Conditions on Mars?**

Mars is the planet the space scientists plan to visit first. Spacecraft have already flown by and taken pictures. The next step in the program will be to send unmanned spacecraft to make tests similar to those made on the Moon. Then astronauts will probably be landed there.

Scientists have believed for many years that Mars is the planet in our solar system most likely to have life on it. It is probably the most like our planet Earth. There are several important differences, however. Although, Mars is tipped on its axis at about the same angle as Earth, it takes 687 days to orbit the Sun. Therefore, although its seasons are much like those on Earth, they are twice as long.

Studies of the Martian atmosphere show that there is not much water on the planet. Astronomers can see white polar caps which get larger in winter and apparently melt in summer. These white polar caps are probably just frost. There does not seem to be enough water to cause large snow fields as we have on Earth.

The Mariner 4 spacecraft flew by Mars and took pictures and made studies. These showed that the atmosphere is mostly of carbon dioxide, nitrogen, and argon and is very thin. It is about the same as our atmosphere would be 20 miles up. No oxygen was found in the atmosphere.

**Mars**

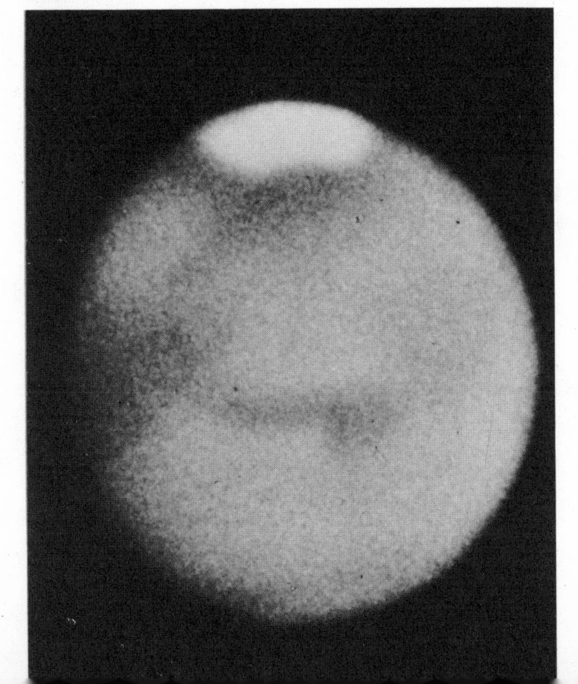

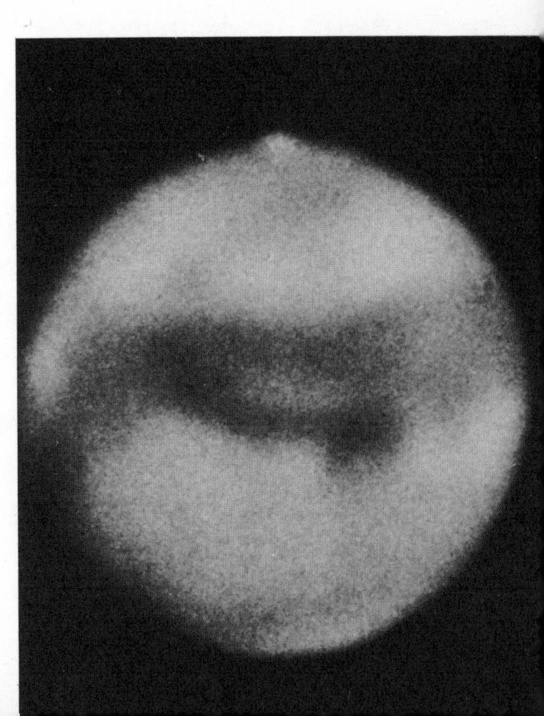

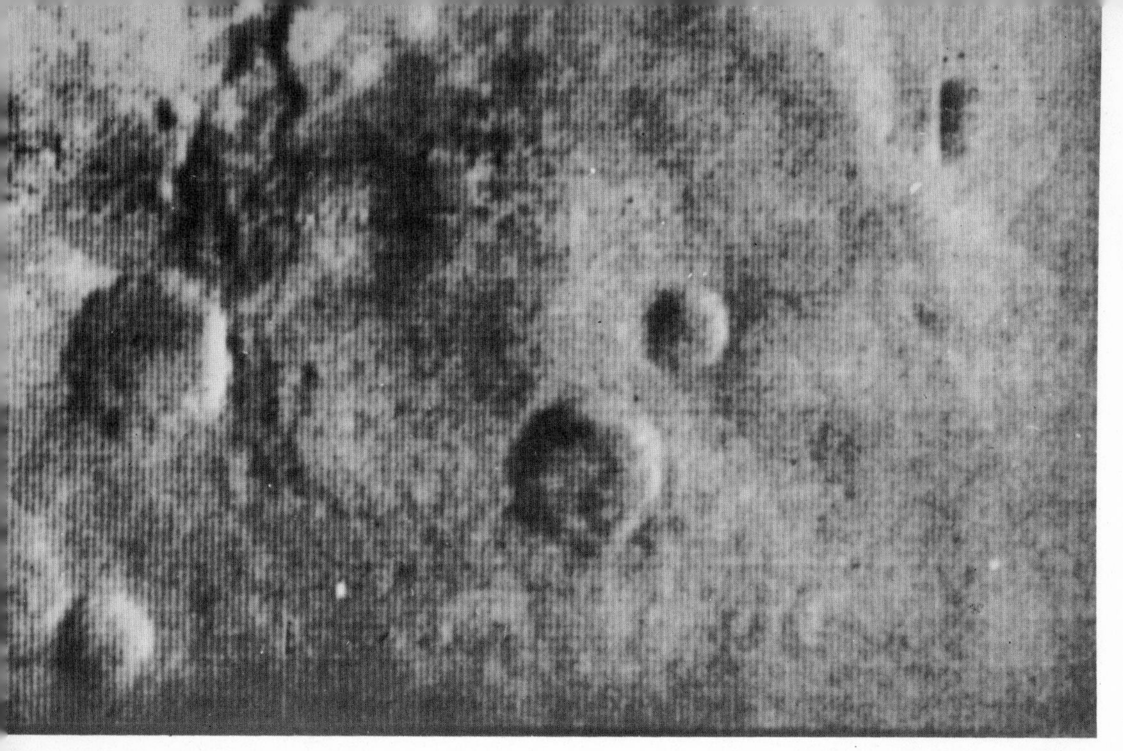

**Surface of Mars**

The photographs that Mariner 4 took were of only about 1 percent of the surface. The part that was photographed looked much like the surface of the Moon.

The instruments on the spacecraft also showed no magnetic field. Scientists believe this means that Mars does not have iron in its core which would cause a magnetic field such as Earth has.

### What Is Known About Jupiter?

The planet Jupiter is quite different from the inner planets, Mercury, Venus, Earth, and Mars. It is much larger and much less dense. If you remember, the chart showed that Jupiter is only a little more dense than water. This probably means that the planet has much hydrogen and helium which are very lightweight elements. These are the elements which make up the Sun to a large extent. Jupiter has apparently changed little since the solar system began. Astronomers are not sure whether the surface is solid or not.

One feature which is different on Jupiter is the Great Red Spot. No one knows what the spot is, but, although it changes color and location, it is always there. Astronomers have different theories about what it is, but no one knows for sure.

It is impossible to see the surface of Jupiter. It is covered with clouds of ammonia crystals. Its atmosphere also contains hydrogen and methane gas. This shows up in telescopes here on Earth as bright and dark bands. Some of the bands seem to rotate faster than others.

### What Is Known About Saturn?

In many ways, the planet Saturn is much like Jupiter. It is not as large, but it is larger than the other planets. It is not dense. In fact, its density is even less than that of Jupiter. It is less dense than water. The low density is caused by the large amounts of hydrogen and helium found there.

**Jupiter**

Both Jupiter and Saturn make one full rotation in about 10 hours. Jupiter is just a little faster. Saturn has light and dark bands like Jupiter. The thing that makes Saturn differ from any of the other planets are the rings that rotate around it. They are probably made of ice crystals. Recently, a new ring was detected, bringing the total to four. This very faint ring is the farthest out and has a diameter of about 340,000 miles.

### What Is Known About the Outer Planets?

Not much is known about the distant planets of Uranus, Neptune, and Pluto because they are too far away to be seen clearly. These planets were not known to ancient astronomers. Neptune and Pluto were only discovered because nearby planets were pulled out of their orbits slightly, showing that something was affecting them. Pluto is different because it is so small. It is so far from the Sun that it is very cold, perhaps -400 degrees F.

There are a few facts that make these planets seem different. Most of the planets seem to revolve in an almost vertical position. Not Uranus, however. Its axis is in an almost horizontal position, so that it rotates like a barrel rolling on its side.

**Saturn**

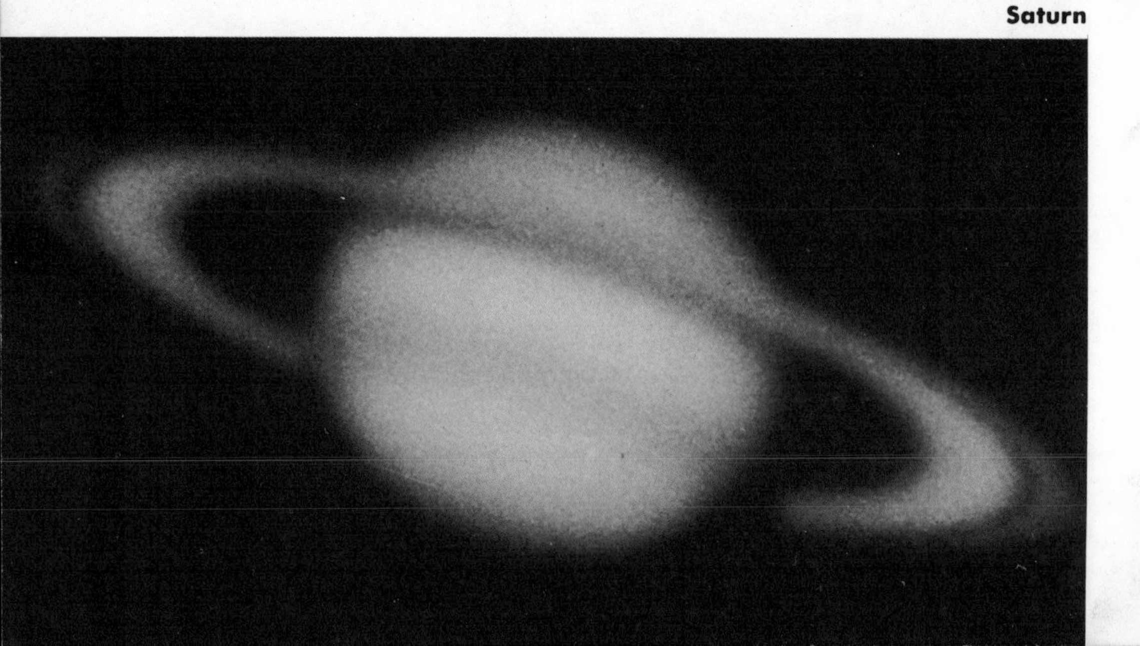

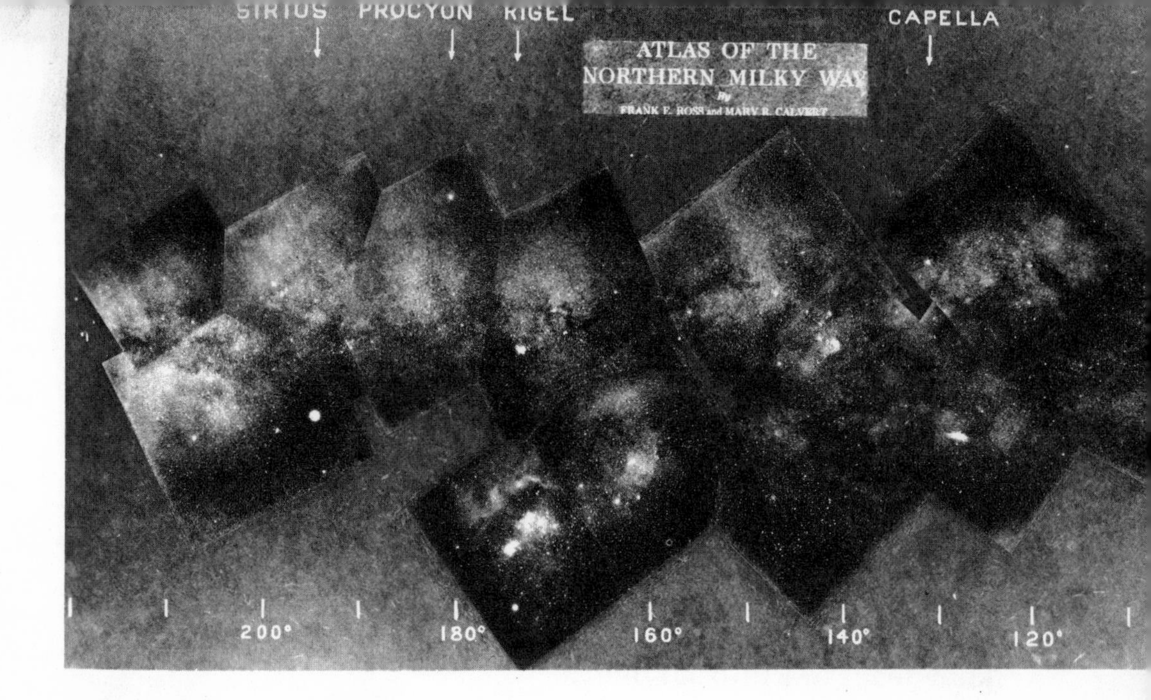


**Where Is Our Solar System in the Universe?**

You have read that our Sun is really only a medium-sized star. Our solar system is probably not very large compared to other solar systems, although it is much more important to us than the others.

Our solar system is a part of a large group of stars called the Milky Way Galaxy. Many of the stars in this large group probably have far more planets than our Sun has. Besides our galaxy, there are many more galaxies visible to astronomers with powerful telescopes. These galaxies are too far away for astronomers to see whether the stars in them have planets. Even the stars of our own galaxy are too far away for us to detect many planets, but a number have been discovered.

You have seen that our planets travel around our Sun. But our Sun is moving toward the star Vega at 12 miles per second, and all the stars of our galaxy turn through space. Our galaxy also rotates, taking about 200 million years for one complete turn. As for the billions of galaxies, most of them are moving away from each other.

## Things to Think About

1. What is meant by the term "escape velocity"? What is escape velocity from the Earth?

2. Why don't we know more about Venus? Why is our knowledge of Pluto so slight?

3. What did Mariner 4 reveal about Mars?

4. Which planet rotates differently from the others? How is its rotation different?

5. Look at the speed at which the planets revolve. What statement of fact can be made about this?

6. Which planets are the largest? Which ones are the least dense? Do you think there might be a connection?

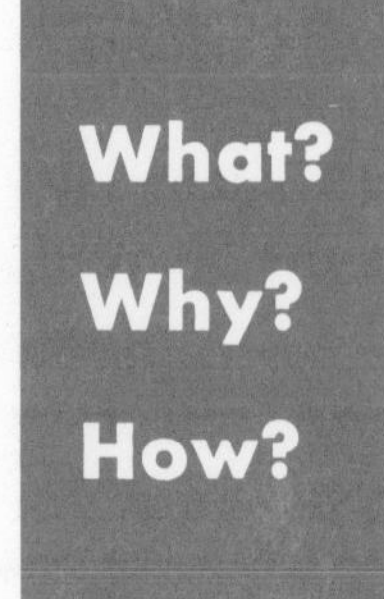


Which planet would you like most to visit? What would you expect to find there? What would the surface be like? Would you expect to find living things there? How would you know if they were living? What would you have to take with you?

# COMETS, METEORS, AND ASTEROIDS

There are many other wanderers in space besides the planets and the moons. These are the comets, meteors, and asteroids, which are too small to be called planets.

Most of the larger meteors and asteroids are revolving around the Sun in an area between Mars and Jupiter.

*Meteorites*, which are meteors that have fallen to Earth, may tell us much about the rest of the solar system. Even these small pieces of matter may have clues as to whether or not there are living things in the solar system. We may learn the kinds of materials that are in the other planets.

We may not learn as much about the solar system from the comets, but they are interesting celestial bodies. Ancient people were frightened by these moving bodies with their fiery tails which came only once in a while and disappeared again. They thought comets brought bad luck.

**What Is a Comet?**

Once upon a time, the appearance of comets was regarded as a bad sign. It could be a warning of war or sickness or bad luck for someone who was planning some big project. Some people, of course, believe even today that some comet or some planet or star combination means good or bad luck for certain people. Of course, if a comet should strike Earth it could be bad luck, but this is not likely to happen. Besides, most of a comet is its tail, and this is a thin gaseous material. If Earth should pass through this thin tail, we would probably not even be aware of the event. In fact, in 1910, Earth did pass through the tail of Halley's comet, and only the astronomers knew that it was happening.

The head of a comet is much different from the tail. Its head consists of a large collection of particles, with some rather large solid chunks of iron and stone. Yet, Earth, through its history of some 4 1/2 billion years, much have met the heads of many comets. It has come through in good condition, although many strong hits must have been experienced. Generally what happens in such cases is that a great fireworks is observed in the sky -- a spectacular display of meteors of "shooting stars." It is the result of the burning of the solid pieces of the head of the comet or some meteors as they enter our atmosphere and burn before reaching the surface.

While a comet is far away from us, we cannot see it. However, as it nears the Sun, much of the small particle material begins to evaporate because of the increased radiation pressure from the Sun. The evaporating material, in thin gaseous form, becomes shiny and begins to glow from action of the Sun's ultraviolet rays. Thus a great tail is born. These tails point into space in the direction opposite to the Sun. As the comet begins to round the Sun, the tail turns always pointing away from the Sun.

Scientists have studied comet tails by finding out what is in the light that they give off. The studies show there is hydrogen, oxygen, carbon, and nitrogen in different combinations. This shows that the tail is made of the lighter elements.

#### What Kind of Path Does a Comet Follow?

Astronomers are not certain whether or not some comets have come to us from another solar system. Recently, the great new comet Ikeya-Seki was observed to have an unusual pathway. It seemed to be that of a *hyperbola* which is an open curve which will not close into a circle or oval. If its path really is an open curve, then the comet came from another solar system, and headed out somewhere into deep space again. Or, we might say that it simply came from outside our own solar system, and after a visit, left it.

In general, however, comets have elliptical orbits. They are under the control of our Sun, and so belong to our own solar system. Some of the elliptical orbits are very long, and so the comet takes a great many years, even centuries, to make a complete trip.

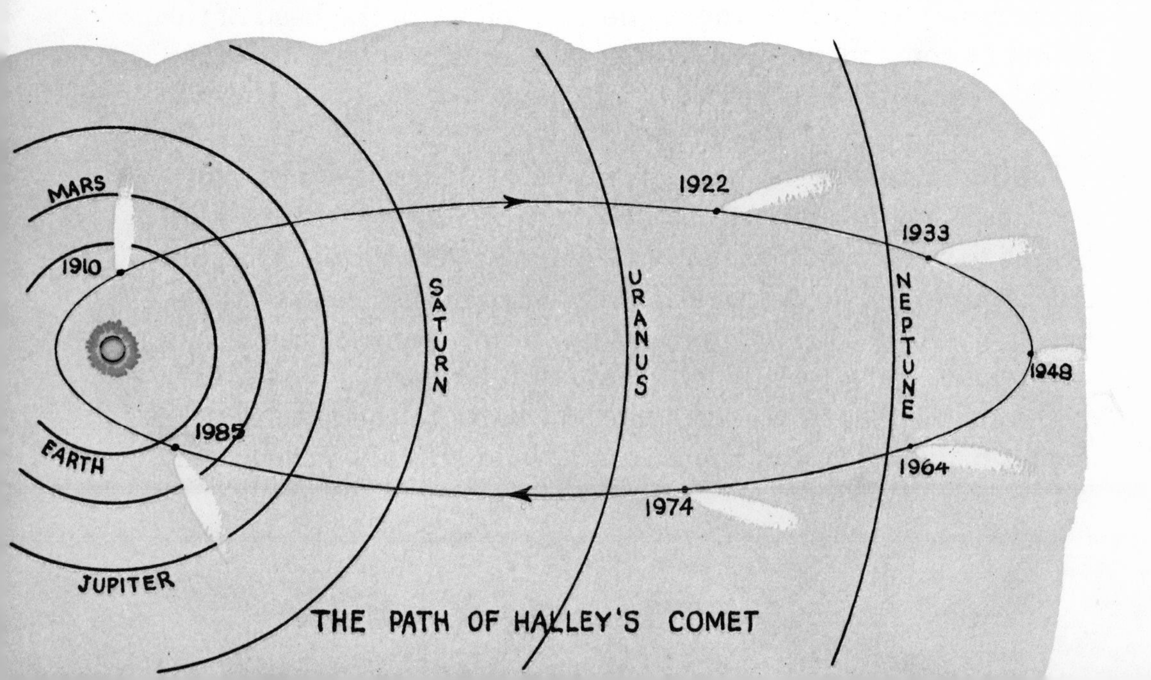


THE PATH OF HALLEY'S COMET

**What Is Halley's Comet?**

Some comets, however, have shorter periods, which is the time of one complete orbit of the Sun. They make regular visits in our sky. One of the best known is Halley's comet, which was named after the English astronomer, Edmund Halley, a friend of Isaac Newton. It was in 1682 that Halley observed a comet, and after following its path, figured out its orbit. He figured it was an ellipse with a period of about 75 years. Halley looked back in the record books and decided that the same comet had appeared in 1531 and 1607. He felt that it would be back in 1758. And it came! It was first seen on Christmas night of 1758, although it had arrived somewhat earlier. Comets are often visible for many weeks. Halley's comet is due back in 1985, since it was last seen in 1910.

A visitor that comes more often is Encke's comet. We can expect it every 3.3 years. However, it does not approach the Sun close enough to grow a long tail. Earthmen must use a telescope to see this visitor.

**What Finally Happens to Comets?**

Since the Sun causes tails on the comets and blows large portions away into space, comets do not exist as long as planets. For some time, Biela's comet orbited the Sun every 6 1/2 years. However, when it came back in 1846, it broke into two separate parts which continued to travel next to each other for a time. At the next return, the two parts had separated to a distance of about 1,200,000 miles. And it didn't come again. But, on the dates it was due, in late November of 1872, 1885 and 1898, the Earth had brilliant showers of meteors, which have been called Andromedes -- because they appear each November 20th in the direction of the group of stars called Andromeda. Astronomers assume that these showers were caused by the clusters of pieces left when the comet broke up completely. With the passing of the years, these showers became smaller and smaller, and now there is little left.

While it seems sure that old comets are broken up, as the years pass, new ones, no doubt, are being constantly created from thin material whirling in space -- for, space is not really a complete vacuum.

**What Are Meteorites?**

A meteorite is what we call a meteor when it lands on Earth. It has burned to a considerable degree as it enters our atmosphere. When meteors begin to burn in our atmosphere, we are apt to call them "shooting stars" and, this, of course, is not correct, although it sounds descriptive and spectacular.

Meteorites come in sizes ranging from tiny particles to enormous chunks weighing many tons. The "iron meteorites," containing mostly iron and nickel, are believed by some scientists to be like the Earth's inner core. If this is so, then one might guess that these meteors and meteorites are pieces caused by an explosion of a planet in the region between Mars and Jupiter. The "stony meteorites" are much like the rocks found on Earth's crust.

**What Causes Asteroids?**

For a long time scientists believed that a planet exploding in the region between Mars and Jupiter could account for the thousands of tiny planets, called asteroids, which orbit the Sun at that distance.

These asteroids are not meteors themselves but, rather, are enormous flying mountains of iron and rock. Many of them are in orbit between the orbits of Mars and Jupiter. They collide with each other, and pieces break off. These collisions produce about one billion tons of meteors and space dust during the course of each year. After a collision, the small pieces or chips from the asteroids may go flying out of orbit. They may head in the direction of Earth and the Moon. Mars has probably been hit even more times than the Earth because it is closer to the asteroid belt.

Diamonds have been found in the center of some of the meteorites which have fallen to the Earth. The presence of diamonds in these meteorites is quite a problem for scientists. On Earth, diamonds are formed only by enormous pressures and very great temperatures deep in the ground. Asteroids are not large enough to have such great pressures and temperatures within them. Only a planet is large enough. This makes scientists wonder again about an exploding planet which might have caused asteroids. These, in turn, would produce meteors through collisions.

A Japanese scientist has found that a single exploding planet could not have caused all the asteroids, considering where they are and the direction they are moving. However, if five planets had collided, exploded, and continued to bump into each other in the region between Mars and Jupiter, this might account for the present asteroid belt.

Some of the asteroids are hundreds of miles in diameter and certainly will be visited by spacemen from Earth in the future. Will astronauts who visit there find that the asteroid has gravity? Since it has mass, it must have some gravity. Will there be much gravity there? Will there be as much as on Earth or the Moon?

Some meteors may not come from the collision of asteriods, but from comets. Although the tail of a comet may be described as a huge bag of dazzling nothing, this description certainly does not apply to the head of the comet. It is a hard core with solid chunks of iron and stone. As comets orbit the Sun, they may shake a vast cluster of meteors loose from the head. These continue in an orbit of their own.

As Earth passes through a point where its orbit passes through the orbit of the meteors, "shooting stars" are seen on Earth. The following year, on the same date (perhaps for two or three days), Earth once more will pass through the same point, and again shooting stars will be seen as some of the meteors pass through Earth's atmosphere. This usually continues year after year.

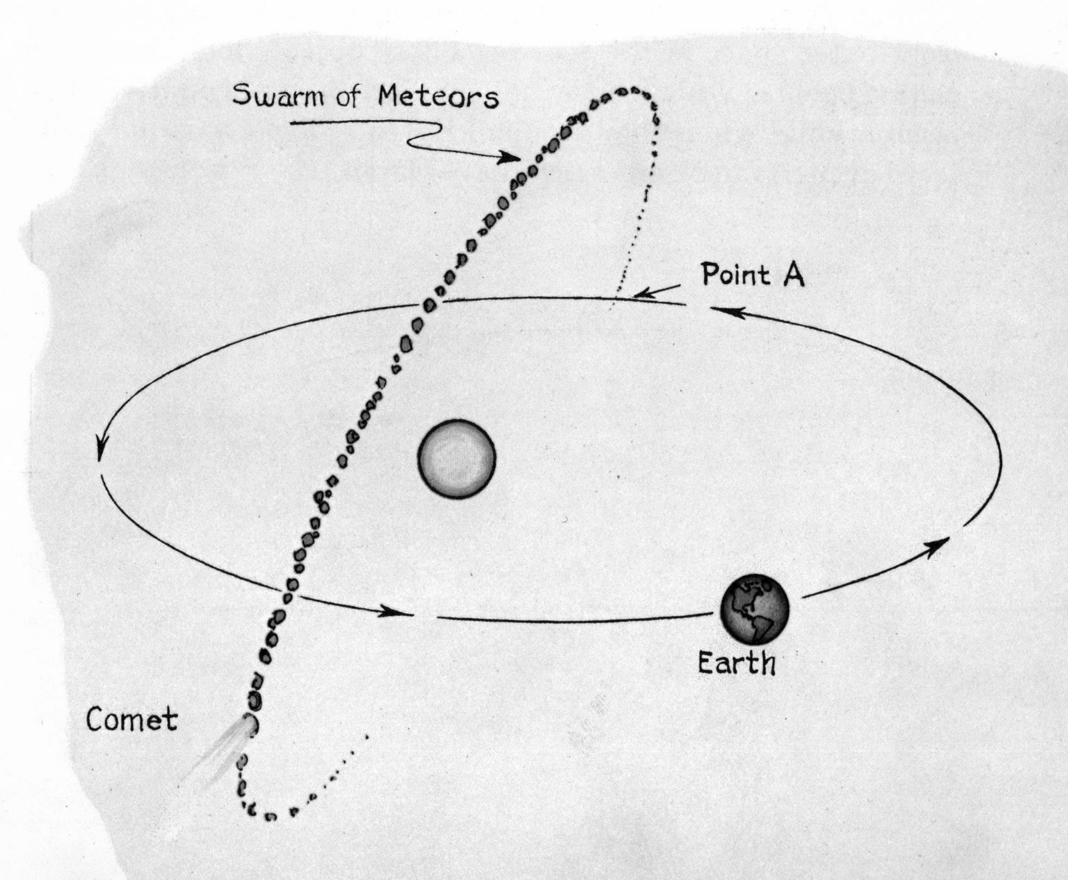

Such points are crossed by Earth a number of times during every year. In the second week of August, we experience such an event, when the meteor swarm of Perseids is crossed. In late October, we get fireworks from the Orionids. During November we catch up with the Leonids, and in early December we get a blast from the Geminids. The Leonid showers of November, 1933 and 1966 were so enormous, where clouds did not obscure the view, that many people on Earth were terrified.

In a number of cases, meteorites seem to contain some fossils of early forms of life. The scientists consider the possibility that the supposed exploded planets in the region between Mars and Jupiter may have had some form of life upon them. Scientists, at present, do not agree about this theory.

**What Is a Tektite?**

Another kind of object which scientists think came to Earth from outer space is the *tektite*. These objects look like little glassy pebbles which were hot, melted drops of matter that became solid when they reached Earth. They are found scattered over eleven or more regions of Earth.

There is still a great question about where tektites came from and how they were formed. They may have been formed when asteroids collided and gave off bits of matter which became so hot they melted. Some scientists believe that the asteroids struck the Earth itself, and the heat of the impact produced the hot, melted droplets, which soon became solid. Still other scientists believe that volcanic eruptions on the Moon hurled lava-like substances to Earth causing tektites.

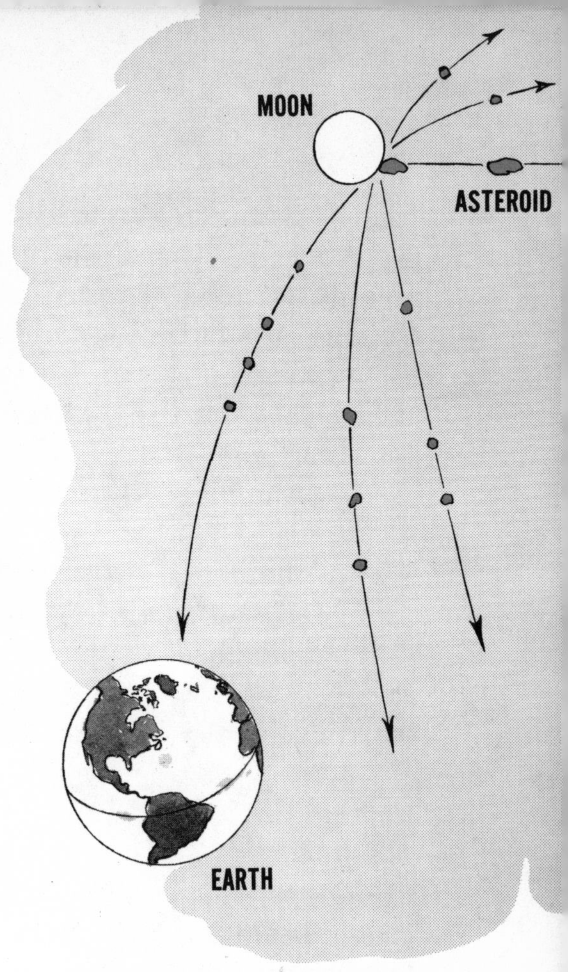


It is possible to estimate the tektite ages by studying their radioactive changes. The studies show that three separate great explosive events in the solar system seem to be responsible for the tektites on Earth. The tektites spread over the Philippines, Indonesia, Southeast Asia, Australia, and Africa's Ivory Coast are about 600,000 years old. The glassy pebbles found in Bohemia are about 8,700,000 years old. The tektites found in Texas and Georgia are about 3,000,000 years old.

One strange thing about the tektites found in Java gives us something to think about. Tektites have been found mixed with bones of the Java Man, who is thought to be one of our most ancient ancestors. The possibility seems to exist, therefore, that the terrific bombardment of 600,000 years ago took the lives of human beings and animals on Earth.

What a wonderful time in which to live! Curious people have always wondered about our planets, the Sun, the Moon, and the stars of the Universe. We are only just beginning to solve the mysteries. Our scientists would like to know more of the way the solar system began. They are wondering whether there are or have ever been living things on other planets. Traveling to and studying on other planets will help solve the mysteries. Will you volunteer to go?

## Things to Think About

1. How is the path of a comet different from that of a planet?

2. How could you tell a comet if you saw one? What are the parts made of?

3. What kind of things can scientists learn from meteorites?

4. Why do diamonds found in meteorites make astronomers wonder if meteors were once part of a planet? Does it mean that the meteors had to have been part of another planet?

5. Why do some meteor showers appear on the same date, year after year?

6. Is space really empty? Why or why not?

**What?**

**Why?**

**How?**

Visit a museum or planetarium where there are exhibits of meteorites and tektites. Look at the exhibits carefully. From the appearance of these, can you tell why scientists have developed the theories they have about where these materials came from and how they were formed? Why does the meteorite look as if it has been burned?

# SUMMARY OF CONCEPTS

1. The solar system consists of the Sun, its nine planets, their moons, and other small objects which orbit the Sun. 7, 30, 33, 75

2. There are several theories of the origin of the solar system, but most agree that the solar system was probably formed from a cloud of gas rotating in space. 8-11

3. The Sun is the center of the solar system. 12-13, 30

4. The Sun is in a state of constant violent action. 15-21, 23

5. The Sun is a hot glowing body which furnishes light and heat for the other objects in the solar system. 15, 22-27, 29

6. The Sun affects the weather of the Earth. 29, 31-32, 36-40

7. The Sun indirectly furnishes the Earth with food and fuel. 29, 34, 35

8. The Moon causes tides on Earth. 47-48

9. Moon and Earth move together around the Sun as they circle each other. 7, 43-45

10. Phases of the Moon are caused by its position in relation to Sun and Earth. 46

11. The study of the Moon is important because it may have clues as to how our solar system began. 51-52

12. The planets of the solar system are quite different from each other in many ways. 59-72

13. Mars is the planet which seems to be most like Earth. 64, 68-69

14. The solar system is only a small part of the celestial bodies visible in the sky. 12, 15

15. All bodies of the universe are in constant motion. 12, 73

16. Comets, meteors, and asteroids are smaller objects in the solar system. 7, 75, 77

17. Most comets have an orbit in the form of a very long ellipse and they are seen only once in a while in our sky. 78-80

18. Comets have a head of solid chunks of iron and stone. Its tail of gaseous material is always pointed away from the Sun. 77-80, 83

19. The largest number of asteroids found in our solar system orbit the sun in a belt between Mars and Jupiter. 75, 81-83

20. The energy from the Sun is caused by a hydrogen-helium reaction. 24-26

21. The planets orbit the Sun because there is a balance between the force of gravity and the tendency of a moving body to continue in a straight line. 12-13

22. The Sun, the Earth, and some planets have magnetic fields. 19-21, 23

23. The Sun will probably last another eight billion years. It will first swell and then as it runs out of helium, it will collapse into a white dwarf. 26-27

24. Scientists have many theories about whether or not there are forms of life on other bodies in the solar system. 53, 68, 69, 84

25. The study of the Moon and some of the planets are a part of the United States space program. 54-56, 59, 66, 67-70

## ACKNOWLEDGEMENTS

**Photos**

Adler Planetarium, 53, 80
Bausch and Lomb, 19
Jet Propulsion Laboratory, 55
Lick Observatory Photograph, COVER, 52
Lowell Observatory Photograph, 69, 72
Mt. Wilson and Palomar Observatory, 16, 67, 71, 79
NASA, 54, 56, 58, 70, 84
Yerkes Observatory, University of Chicago, 73, 76, 81

**Artists**

William L. Marsh
Donald Meighan, 8-9, 22
Berthold Tiedemann, 37


## KEY OPERATIONS AND PROCESSES OF SCIENCE AND THE SCIENTIST

The processes of science have helped men find out much about their world. When a scientist begins an investigation, he is always alert to the meaningful manner in which science seeks answers to questions.

Listed below are some of the operations of science and the page numbers of places in the book where they appear.

## ANSWERS TO OPEN-END QUESTIONS IN "THINGS TO THINK ABOUT" SECTIONS.

CHAPTER 1 (page 14)

1. The Moon is not a planet because it orbits a planet, not the Sun. However, like a planet, it does not give off its own light but shines because of reflected light from the Sun.

5. The explanation of why the Moon orbits the Earth is the same as why the Earth orbits the Sun. The force of gravity of the Earth keeps the Moon from flying off into space because of its forward speed.

**What, Why, How**

A non-moving body falls to the ground because of gravity. If the ball is swung and let loose, it shoots off in a straight line. If you swing the ball on a string, the string represents gravity which keeps it from flying away.

CHAPTER 2 (page 28)

4. We are 93 million miles from the Sun and sometimes it is so hot that we are uncomfortable. If we were only one million miles from the Sun, the water would boil away and Earth would be too hot for living things.

5. From another solar system, our Sun would look like a medium-sized star. The planets might not be visible even with a telescope.

**What, Why, How**

If the telescope is pointing properly, the sunspots will be easy to see. They will look like small, dark spots in the central part of the Sun. If you watch them each day, you will see them move as the Sun rotates. Remember that the image is backwards and upside down. The sunspots really will be moving in the opposite direction from what they seem to be.

## CHAPTER 3 (page 41)

4. If the Earth's axis were not tilted, the Sun's rays would hit the Earth at the same angle all the time, and the seasons would not change.

5. If satellites were used to control the weather, it would probably be difficult to decide which weather would be best for an area. The farmers might want rain for their crops, but someone planning a picnic or a carnival would want clear weather. It would be useful to break up violent storms before they could do much damage.

7. A planet having no tilt to its axis and having no atmosphere would not have seasons or daily changes in weather. However, they would have day and night as the planet rotated, and there would be a great difference in the temperature in the day and night. There would be no atmosphere to protect the surface from the burning rays of the Sun or to become heated and spread to the dark side of the planet.

**What, Why, How**

If you have exactly the same conditions for the two plants, except that one has light and the other does not, the one without light will soon begin to lose its green coloring and then it will die.

**CHAPTER 4** (page 57)

7. People who go to the Moon will need food, water, and oxygen. Since the Moon has none of these, people from Earth will have to carry their own. They may find ways to grow food on the Moon. The Moon is very hot on the sunny side and very cold on the dark side. Ways must be found to control the temperature if man is to live there.

8. Earth would be a large shining object in the Moon's sky because of reflected light from the Sun. It would have phases just as the Moon does as we view it from Earth.

**CHAPTER 5** (page 74)

5. A look at the table on page 60 shows that the further a planet is from the Sun, the longer it takes to revolve. It has a longer way to go but its speed is also less. The further from the Sun, the less is the force of gravity. Therefore, the planet does not need as much speed to balance the force of gravity and to stay in orbit.

**CHAPTER 6** (page 87)

6. Space contains so much gas and space dust that it can hardly be called empty.

**What, Why, How**

Objects which come from outer space and enter our atmosphere become very hot. This is caused by friction with the air molecules. Much of the meteor will burn in the atmosphere because of this heat. If the meteor is large enough a piece may reach Earth. This meteorite will look something like a cinder.

# GLOSSARY

## PRONUNCIATION SYMBOLS



a as in map
ā as in **day**
ä as in **cot**
á as in f**a**ther
aù as in **out**
b as in **baby**
ch as in **chin**
d as in **did**
e as in b**e**d
ē as in eas**y**
f as in cu**ff**
g as in **g**o
h as in **h**at
i as in t**i**p
ī as in s**i**de
j as in **j**ob
k as in **k**in
l as in poo**l**
m as in di**m**
n as in **no**
ŋ as in si**ng**
ō as in b**o**ne
ȯ as in **saw**
ȯi as in **coin**
p as in li**p**
r as in **r**a**r**ity
s as in le**ss**
sh as in **sh**y
t as in **t**ie
th as in **th**in
<u>th</u> as in **th**en
ü as in r**u**le
u̇ as in p**u**ll
v as in gi**v**e
w as in **we**
y as in **y**ard
z as in **z**one
zh as in vi**si**on
ə as in banan**a**, **c**o**llect**

**aphelion** /a-'fēl-yən/ furthest point of planet's, or other object's orbit from Sun. 30

**apogee** /'ap-ə-(,)jē/ point at which the Moon or a satellite is furthest from Earth. 44

**asteroid** /'as-tə-,rȯid/ very small planet. 75

**axis** /'ak-səs/ imaginary line around which Earth turns. 31

**calorie** /'kal-(ə)-rē/ amount of heat needed to raise temperature of one gram of water one degree Centigrade. 23

**celestial** /sə-'les(h)-chəl/ of or relating to the sky. 7

**chromosphere** /'krō-mə-,sfi(ə)r/ thin layer of the Sun between photosphere and corona. 17

**comet** /'käm-ət/ a luminous object which generally orbits the Sun. It has a head of iron and stone and a tail of gases which glow when it nears the Sun. 7

**corona** /kə-'rō-nə/ outer part of the Sun. 17

**deuteron** /'d(y)üt-ə-,rän/ a heavy hydrogen nucleus containing one neutron and one proton. 25

**eclipse** /i-'klips/ the hiding of one celestial body by another closer one. 49

**electron** /i-'lek-,trän/ tiniest particle with a negative charge. 20

**element** /'el-ə-mənt/ a substance which has atoms of only one kind. There are 92 natural elements found on Earth. 10

**ellipse** /i-'lips/ an oval shape. 30

**escape velocity** /is-'kāp və-'läs-ət-ē/ the speed needed to escape from the force of gravity of a planet. 63

**fusion** /'fyü-zhən/ uniting of certain particles such as protons, neutrons, or helium nuclei. 24

**galaxy** /'gal-ək-sē/ a very large group of stars and their solar systems. 73

**hyperbola** /hī-'pər-bə-lə/ open curve which will never close. 78

**magnetic field** /mag-'net-ik fēld/ the area which is affected by presence of a magnet. 19

**meteor** /'mēt-ē-ər/ a small object of stone or iron flying through space. 7

**meterorite** /'mēt-ē-ə-,rīt/ piece of meteor that reaches the surface of the Earth. 52

**moon** /'mün/ a celestial body which orbits a planet. 7

**nucleus** /'n(y)ü-klē-əs/ central part of an atom. 24

**orbit** /'ȯr-bət/ the path one celestial body takes around another. 9; moving of one body around another. 12

**panspermia** /pan-'spər-mē-ə/ a theory that life may spread from one celestial body to another by the transfer of spores through space. 53

**perigee** /'per-ə-(,)jē/ point at which a moon or satellite of the Earth is nearest Earth. 44

**perihelion** /per-ə-'hēl-yən/ closest point to Sun of any planet or other body orbiting the Sun. 30

**photosphere** /'fōt-(,)ō-'sfi(ə)r/ the part of the Sun which surrounds the hot core. 17

**photosynthesis** /'fōt-ō-'sin(t)-thə-səs/ process in which green plants grow food by using sunlight, water, carbon dioxide. 34

**plage** /'pläzh/ bright, hot region on the Sun. 17

**planet** /'plan-ət/ a celestial body which moves in an orbit around a sun. 7

**precession** /prē-'sesh-ən/ slow turning of the axis of a spinning body so that it traces a double cone in space. 32

**prominence** /'präm-(ə)-nən(t)s/ a mass of gas which rises from the surface of the Sun. 17

**proton** /'prō-,tän/ particle with one positive charge. 20

**protoplanet** /prōt-ə-'plan-ət/ huge whirling mass of gas rotating around a sun. Thought to be the start of a planet. 11

**spectrum** /'spek-trəm/ a band of colors which form from sunlight. 19; range of electromagnetic waves of energy given off by the Sun. 22

**spores** /'spō(ə)rz/ small bodies produced by some plants and animals that can develop into new plants and animals. 53

**tektite** /'tek-,tīt/ a small glassy pebble thought to be from the Moon. 84

**universe** /'yü-nə-,vers/ all the celestial bodies, everything that exists. 54

# INDEX